Edward Christian

An Examination of Precedents and Principles

From which it appears that an impeachment is determined by a dissolution of

Parliament

Edward Christian

An Examination of Precedents and Principles
From which it appears that an impeachment is determined by a dissolution of Parliament

ISBN/EAN: 9783337152147

Printed in Europe, USA, Canada, Australia, Japan

Cover: Foto ©Suzi / pixelio.de

More available books at **www.hansebooks.com**

AN EXAMINATION

OF

PRECEDENTS

AND

PRINCIPLES;

FROM WHICH IT APPEARS

That an IMPEACHMENT is determined
by a DISSOLUTION of PARLIAMENT.

WITH AN

APPENDIX,

In which all the PRECEDENTS are collected.

The SECOND EDITION, much enlarged.

By EDWARD CHRISTIAN, Esq.
BARRISTER,
And PROFESSOR of the LAWS of England, in the University
of CAMBRIDGE.

LONDON:
PRINTED FOR J. STOCKDALE, PICCADILLY, AND
J. DEIGHTON, N° 274, HIGH-HOLBORN.
M.DCC.XCI.

FROM my situation in the University of Cambridge, I think it my duty not to be uninformed upon any question which concerns the Constitution of this country. That consideration alone impelled me to institute the present Examination. Many gentlemen of late have deprecated the discussion of abstract questions, and have declared that such speculations are mischievous and dangerous; but I have never heard any reason assigned for their alarms. It certainly would be inconsistent with their dignity, and a waste of that time which might be more profitably employed, if the two Houses of Parliament or Courts of Justice should be occupied in the solution of problems and subtleties which were not necessary for the decision of any particular case.

But

But all science consists of abstract questions. There are many who are perfectly acquainted with astronomy, who never made an observation with a quadrant or a telescope: and there are many who have a profound knowledge of the Constitution and the Laws of England, who never had the honour of a seat in the Senate, or the misfortune to be engaged in a law-suit. It happens to be peculiarly my occupation to investigate abstract questions; and it certainly ought to be considered immaterial to the extension of science, whether a question is proposed with the name of Warren Hastings, or with that of Titius or Sempronius. Those who have most examined the English government, will be the most convinced, allowing for a few defects incident to every human institution, that it preserves inviolate all the Rights of Men, which men in society ought to enjoy, or, if they are wise, would desire to enjoy; that it is such a system of liberty and justice, that the communication of its principles must necessarily give stability to its existence.

It is a common obfervation, that the prefent important queftion depends upon the principles of the Conftitution, and not upon the principles of law; and that we lawyers have narrow and contracted habits of reafoning, which difqualify us from forming a correct judgment upon fubjects of fuch magnitude: and we find, that when a precedent, or a rule of law, is fuggefted by a profeffional gentleman, as an impediment to the profecution of certain favourite meafures, the impatience which is felt from the reftraint, is dignified with the name of a liberal way of thinking. But perhaps the country owes much to this *illiberality* of the lawyers, as it prevents, in no inconfiderable degree, both *Reafons of State*, and the *Quod placuit* of politicians, from introducing a chaos into our government. From our employment, unaccuftomed to yield our affent without examination, we are not eafily feduced by eloquence, nor frightened by the anathemas of combined power, into acquiefcence, where no arguments have been brought to convince. It is rather remarkable,

remarkable, that though the *constitution* is the most favourite term in the English language, yet no word has been less honoured by explanation. I have never seen, in any book of science, either ancient or modern, any attempt to give a definition of it, except in Mr. Paley's Principles of Moral and Political Philosophy. Nothing that flows from his pen can be undeserving of attention and respect. "By the constitution of a coun-
" try is meant, says he, so much of its law as
" relates to the designation and form of the
" legislature; the rights and functions of the
" several parts of the legislative body; the
" construction, office, and jurisdiction of
" courts of justice. The constitution is
" one principal division, section, or title of
" the code of public laws; distinguished
" from the rest only by the superior im-
" portance of the subject of which it
" treats. Therefore the terms *constitu-
" tional* and *unconstitutional*, mean *legal* and
" *illegal*. The distinction and the ideas,
" which these terms denote, are founded
" in the same authority with the law of
" the

" the land upon any other subject, and
" to be ascertained by the same inquiries.
" In England the system of public juris-
" prudence is made up of acts of parlia-
" ment, of decisions of courts of law,
" and of immemorial usages : conse-
" quently these are the principles of
" which the English Constitution itself
" consists; the sources from which all our
" knowledge of its nature and limitations
" is to be deduced, and the authorities
" to which all appeal ought to be made,
" and by which every constitutional doubt
" and question can alone be decided. This
" plain and intelligible definition is the
" more necessary to be preserved in our
" thoughts, as some writers upon the sub-
" ject *absurdly confound what is constitutio-*
" *nal with what is expedient*; pronouncing
" forthwith a measure to be unconstitu-
" tional, which they adjudge in any
" respect to be detrimental or dangerous;
" whilst others again ascribe a kind of a
" transcendent authority, or mysterious
" sanctity, to the constitution, as if it
" were

"were founded in some higher original
"than that which gives force and obli-
"gation to the ordinary laws and statutes
"of the realm, or were inviolable on any
"other account than its intrinsic uti-
"lity."*

In proof of this excellent definition, we use the word Constitution, when we speak of the King, Parliament, Courts of Justice, Juries, and the Magistracy of the Country; but the rules relative to private or inferior subjects, as wills, promissory notes, and bills of exchange, are included under the more general denomination of Law: but we may always substitute law for the constitution, being only a more comprehensive term; for the law controls every member of the government: even the King himself is a subject to the Law—*Rex est sub lege, quia lex facit Regem*, is one of our sacred maxims. Every constitutional question is necessarily a legal question: who, then, are the best qualified to afford information

* Vol. II. p. 190.

mation upon conftitutional fubjects; thofe who have traced the Nile to its fource, and who have fpent years in travelling along its ftream, or thofe who in general have only fkimmed acrofs its furface, and have contented themfelves with a tranficnt admiration of its beauties?

We have lately, from a general concurrence in opinion, been charged with a combination, and an *efprit de Corps*. Whatever may be the truth of our principles, the coincidence of our conclufions proves the confiftency of our reafoning. With regard to myfelf, I can declare that I fent the firft edition of this pamphlet to the prefs without any communication or confultation with any perfon whatever but my bookfeller, and without knowing the opinion of any individual from the higheft to the loweft of the profeffion. But I now think it no mean honour to have .... a volunteer, and to have lent my feeble aid to that independent phalanx of veterans in the profeffion, feſſion, who, upon this occaſion, have ſtood firm in the defence of what they are convinced is the Conſtitution and the Law of England.

AN

EXAMINATION

OF

PRECEDENTS, &c.

AN important Conſtitutional Queſtion at preſent engages the attention and expectation of the Public, in which the intereſts of an Individual, and the privileges of both Houſes of Parliament, are materially concerned; viz. Whether an Impeachment abates, and is determined, by a diſſolution of the Parliament in which it was commenced; or, whether the proceedings in the Houſe of Lords remain ſo unaltered and undiſturbed, that the Trial can be continued after the diſſolution, juſt as it could have been after an adjournment or prorogation in the laſt Parliament. This is a point which, ſolely for his own information, and the gratification of his curiosity, the author of this Examination was induced to investigate; and, the result of his researches, he conceives, will not be unuseful or uninstructive to his Profession, or to the Public.

With regard to that Gentleman who has been charged by the Commons of Great-Britain with high crimes and misdemeanors, the author protests that he has been so incurious to the circumstances of the trial, that his mind has not the least bias or inclination to induce him to pronounce, like the Peers, Guilty or Not guilty, upon his honour. But, even if the defendant were guilty of the charges exhibited against him, in the fullest extent, no one, who has a due regard and proper veneration for the English Constitution, would wish to see the two Houses of Parliament transgress the bounds of their jurisdiction prescribed by the Law, in order to inflict a punishment commensurate to his crimes.

The first object of the laws, is the protection of the innocent; and the best way to secure this, is by the punishment of the guilty. For this end, judicatures have been established, and magistrates appointed; but where these magistrates disregard the authority delegated to them, such confusion must be the consequence, that the innocent will suffer, and the guilty escape unpunished.

It is the transcendent excellence of the British government, that the whole is comprehended and embraced by the Law. Those blessings of liberty which we enjoy, we owe to that Law, which accurately defines the prerogatives of the King, the extent of the privileges of the two Houses of Parliament, and the power and authority of every subordinate magistrate in the kingdom.

These prerogatives, privileges, and powers, constitute no inconsiderable portion of the Rights of Englishmen: from a due exercise of these, the security and tranquillity of the whole are produced: and though cases of great delinquency may perhaps sometimes exist, which the arm of the Law cannot reach, which it can neither punish nor prevent; yet I should say, in the strong and sensible language of Sir Martin Wright, " * That these " are particular and single inconveniences; " and the policy of the law of England, " and indeed the true principles of all " government, will rather suffer many " private inconveniences than introduce " one public mischief."

Since the commencement of the present Impeachment, a monstrous doctrine has been urged, which, if established, would arm the House of Lords with a despotic power, and might eventually prove fatal to our liberty and constitution; which is, that they are not bound, like inferior courts, by the rigid and inflexible rules of evidence, but that they might admit, at their discretion,

* Foster, 29.

cretion, any species of information which they might think necessary for the investigation of truth.

But I trust that the Lords will always have wisdom and virtue to reject such pernicious propositions, and will remember that, in their character of judges, it is their province *jus dicere*, and not *jus dare*.*

The rules of evidence, like the rules of morality, are presumed to be founded in the best sense possible, in reason and wisdom matured and confirmed by the experience of ages; and, in all criminal proceedings, both in the highest and lowest

---

* This may be thought to be expressed with an unbecoming vehemence. It is a doctrine which I have frequently been obliged to reprobate among the circle of my friends; and I introduce it here, to enforce that universal principle, that the spirit and substance of English liberty consists in the strict adherence to rules and the letter of the law; and the more we introduce of arbitrary discretion, the more we shall approximate to the detestable maxims of the Eastern Governments.

lowest courts, whether at the Quarter-sessions, or in the High Court of Parliament, and in the Court of the Lord High Steward, are, and ought to be precisely the same.

And my Lord Coke solemnly cautions Parliaments " * to leave all causes to be " measured by the golden and streight " metwand of the Law, and not by the " uncertain and crooked cord of discre-" tion."

But though each of the two Houses of Parliament may do many acts, from which there is no remedy or appeal, yet I trust that they will always have such a conscientious regard to the extent of their privileges and jurisdiction, that they will never adopt the maxim, That they can do no wrong,—because they can do wrong with impunity.

Indeed, ever since the Revolution, the two Houses of Parliament have been scrupulously

* 4 Inst. 41.

puloufly anxious to keep within the limits of their authority; and if we did not perceive this folicitude in the two Houfes, " to meafure their conduct by the golden " metwand of the Law," the people of England would have much more to apprehend from the improper exercife of the privilege of Parliament, than of the prerogative of the Crown.

We hear much of the *Lex et Confuetudo Parliamenti*; and it has always been reprefented as a myftery beyond the comprehenfion of vulgar, uninitiated minds: that it is " * *ab omnibus quærenda, à* " *multis ignorata, à paucis cognita;*" and that there is a " † particular cunning in " it, which even our Judges are unac- " quainted with." But, as the judicature of the Houfe of Lords is always open, and as all the proceedings which are in exiftence, of both Houfes, have been publifhed, I have never been able to fee any
reafon

---
* 1 Inft. 11 b.
‡ Mr. J. Powell, 2 Lord Raymond, 944.

reason why the Law of Parliament should be more unintelligible than the *Lex Coronæ*, which has been so freely and amply discussed, or more inexplicable than the proceedings of the inferior courts. The usage and custom of Parliament constitutes the Law of Parliament, which is part of the common law of the land, or part of the *Lex et Consuetudo Angliæ*.

Many of the proceedings of Parliament have been introduced by modern statutes, as by Grenville's act, the Septennial act, &c. and where they depend only upon usage, this usage, like all the common law, may be presumed to have had as valid and as respectable an origin.

But this *Lex et Consuetudo Parliamenti* is best understood, as my Lord Coke declares, " * by reading the Judgments and
" Records of Parliament at large, and the
" Journals of the House of Lords, and
" the book of the Clerk of the House of
" Commons."

* 4 Inst. 23.

In addition to the orders and precedents which may be found there, conclusions, in doubtful cases, may be drawn from principles; viz. by considering the nature of the original constitution of Parliaments, their history and progress, their relation and analogy to other parts of the Law, and the convenience and inconvenience of the different determinations proposed; for, as all Law must be supposed to have general convenience for its object, where there is no other consideration to guide the judgment, that determination must be presumed to be the best law, which is the most convenient.

Upon this Question respecting the Impeachment, both Precedents and Principles compel me to conclude that the Impeachment is determined by the dissolution.

It is not now a question of the first impression; but it has been frequently agitated, upon the most solemn occasions, in the two Houses of Parliament.

No less than four Committees in the House of Lords have been appointed within the space of forty years, to search for precedents upon this subject. These Committees made their inquiries in times of great anxiety and expectation, and have given abundant proofs of their attention and industry.

But I shall here briefly state, in chronological arrangement, the substance of these * Orders and Precedents; and shall afterwards make a few observations upon each of them.

† 11 *March*, 1672.—It was referred, by the House of Lords, to a Committee, to consider whether writs of error and appeals continued in *statu*

---

* Vide those Precedents at length, in the Appendix.

† *Nota*.—At that time the legal year begun on the 25th of March; so that when December and March, till the 25th, &c. are mentioned of the same year, December will precede March.

statu quo unto the next seffion of Parliament.

29 *March*, 1673.—The Lords Committees produce feveral precedents from the time of Edward I, and report that bufineffes depending in *one Parliament, or Seffion of Parliament,* have been continued to the *next Seffion of the fame Parliament,* and the proceedings thereupon have remained in the fame ftate in which they were left, when laft in agitation.

11 *March*, 1678.—It is referred to the Lords Committees, whether appeals can be proceeded upon after the diffolution.

17 *March*, 1678.—It is referred to the Committee to confider appeals as in the preceding Order; and alfo to confider the ftate of Impeachments brought

brought up at laſt Parliament (a diſſolution having intervened).

19 *March*, 1678.—The Lords Committees report that appeals and writs of error continue in *ſtatu quo*, and that the *diſſolution does not alter the ſtate of the Impeachments;* and it was ordered accordingly.

22 *May* 1685.—It was reſolved, that the preceding Order, of the 19 *March* 1678, ſhould be *reverſed and annulled as to Impeachments.*

5 *April*, 1690.—An Order was made to take into conſideration, whether Impeachments continue from Parliament to Parliament.

7 *July*, 1690.—The Parliament prorogued, and no report made.

2 *October*, 1690.—The Parliament met after prorogation.

6 *October*, 1690.—A Committee was appointed to inspect and consider precedents whether Impeachments continue in *statu quo* from Parliament to Parliament.

30 *October*, 1690.—The Committee report various precedents (vide the Appendix, p. xiii); upon consideration of which, and former Orders, the House of Lords discharged Lord Peterborough, and Lord Salisbury, who had been impeached before the dissolution, from their bail.

22 *May*, 1717.—It was ordered, that all the Lords should be a Committee to search for and report such precedents as relate to the continuance of Impeachments from Session to Session, or from Parliament to Parliament.

25 *May*, 1717.—The Lords Committees make a very full report of predents, from the year 1660; which being read, it was propofed to refolve, That the Impeachment of the Commons, againft the Earl of Oxford, is determined by the intervening *prorogation*.
It was refolved in the negative.

So here are the Reports of four Committees in the Houfe of Lords, befides the important vote of that Houfe, on the 22d of May, 1685, when no Committee had been previoufly appointed; and it appears that for forty years this Queftion muft have serioufly engaged the attention of that Houfe; and if a material cafe, upon the fubject, could have been difcovered by any of the Lords, it would certainly have been confidered a valuable prize.

The inftructions to the firft Committee, on the 11th of *March*, 1672, relate only to appeals and writs of error. But in the Report

Report, the Lords Committees state various precedents from the time of Edward I. from which it appears, that they had not confined their inquiries to appeals and writs of error, but had extended them to every species of judicial proceeding before Parliament; for they cite two instances of criminal proceedings, of which that of the Archbishop of Canterbury is one of the most important cases which I have seen referred to, or have found, in the Rolls of Parliament in ancient times.

* In the 15th year of Edward the Third, the Archbishop of Canterbury had, of his own accord, stated in Parliament, that he had been defamed throughout the kingdom and elsewhere, and prayed the King that he might be arraigned before the Peers, which the King granted. Afterwards, certain of the Lords were appointed to hear the answers of the Archbishop; and if the answers should be *convenables*, the King of his good grace would excuse him. " Et
" en cas qu'il semble au Roi & à son Con-
" seil,

* Vide Appendix, p. xxxvii.

" seil, que meismes les respons ne sont myc
" suffisantz, adonques les ditz respons fer-
" ront *débatuz en preschein Parlement, &*
" *illoques eut juggement rendu.*"

And in a Parliament or Session held two years afterwards, 17 Ed. III. every thing touching the arraignment of the Archbishop is annulled and cancelled, as not being reasonable or true. From this, it certainly appears, that the arraignment and answer might be made in one *Parlement*, and that judgment might be given in the next.

But I shall shew by and by, that the word *Parlement*, or Parliament, was applied always to a Session, and not confined to a Parliament, according to the modern acceptation of the word. But upon looking into Prynne's Brevia Parliamentaria Rediviva, I find there is a strong presumption, that the whole of the proceedings in the Archbishop's case were transacted in what we we call the fame Parliaments, or that the proceedings were not continued after a diffolution. When Mr. Prynne informs us that there was a new writ of fummons, we are fure that there has been a diffolution; but where no writ is found in his collection, it certainly is not equally conclufive that no diffolution or new election has intervened, becaufe all the writs of that year may have been loft :—he tells us, that part of many of the bundles of writs, as for inftance the writs for Cornwall or Cambridgefhire, are decayed or wanting; but if he found any writs remaining for any other county, it is clear that there had been a new election. I do not know, (though perhaps it may be very well known by others) that it appears either from parliamentary records, or from any general or local hiftory, that in fact there were elections in ancient times, of which the writs of fummons do not appear in Prynne's Catalogues. It appears from Prynne, that writs iffued for a new Parliament tefted;

An. 15. *Edw. III. apud Woodstock*, 3 *die Martii*; that his next writ is tested; *An.* 17. *Edw. III. apud Kenelworth*, 26 *die Decembris:* and it also appears from the Rolls of Parliament, that the Parliament in which the Archbishop complains, was held at Westminster 15 days after Easter; the Archbishop's arraignment is concluded in a Parliament held at Westminster 15 days after Easter, in the 17th of Edw. III. the new writ does not issue till the 26th of December in that year: so that the proceedings with respect to the Archbishop may have been in one Parliament prorogued, or in different sessions of the same Parliament: and, from these dates, as nothing appears to the contrary, it is fair to presume it. And before the reader has got to the end of this pamphlet, I trust he will have some reason to suppose, that the Parliament was prorogued and not dissolved, because the Archbishop's arraignment was pending and unfinished *.

The

---

* Vide the Archbishop's case at length. Appendix, xxxvi.

The cafe of Hugh Suffolk, called Hugh Faftolf in the Roll of Parliament, 51 Ed. III. is this:—The Record ftates, that *fur le fyn du darrein Parlement*, he had been impeached by the malice and hatred of fome of his neighbours, his enemies, of extortion, and other mifconduct; that fpecial commiffioners had been appointed to try him, and that by feventeen inquefts he had been acquitted: the Commons, therefore, pray the Lords, that the faid Hugh might be reftored to his good fame and name. This Parliament fat at Weftminfter 15 days after St. Hilary; and, according to Prynne, the writ of fummons is tefted Ann. 50, E. III. apud Havering, 1 die Decembris. But the darrein Parlement, which this Roll in the 51 Ed. III. perpetually refers to, was held in the 50 Ed. III. in April, and which, by the Roll itfelf, appears to have been diffolved: and this correfponds with Prynne's writs. So this proceeding was unqueftionably in a new Parliament. But it cannot be confidered as a continuation of the former extraordinary profecution; but it is an original petition: " q'il ent fuft ore en ceft Parlement, " reftorez à fa bone fame et bone loos par " mefme, la manere come il eft trovez " devante les Juftices."

There are many inftances in the Rolls of Parliament, where the fame perfons are named in different records. But we muft always confider whether they are continuations of the original proceedings, or whether they are not frefh impeachments, bills of attainder, or reverfals of attainder, or original proceedings of themfelves; and from what I have feen in every inftance where the fame perfon is named after a diffolution, it is a frefh or original proceeding (except writs of error, which I fhall fhortly take notice of), as in this Roll of Parliament there are a number of petitions to the King to pardon feveral perfons therein fpecified, who, as they ftate, had been impeached wrongfully, and of great malice, in the laft Parliament. Thefe petitions are certainly as diftinct proceedings, from the
petitions

petitions of impeachment in the former Parliament, as the bill to reverse Lord Stafford's attainder was distinct from his impeachment.

But before we proceed farther, it will be absolutely necessary to enquire into the original signification of the word *Parliament*.—I will not trouble the reader with the foolish and ridiculous etymologies which have been given of this word. It simply means a council, or conference, without any regard to the manner by which the members of that conference are convened.

* My Lord Coke, somehow or other, had become possessed of a manuscript, entitled, " Modus tenendi Parliamentum, " tempore regis Edwardi, filii regis Ethel- " dredi, &c." which he boasted of, as if he had found the philosopher's stone. It pretended to give a description of the constitution of Parliaments before the Conquest; which Selden, Spelman, and Prynne, both

from

* Vide 4 Inst. 12.

from feudal principles, and from facts, were convinced did not exift till long after the Conqueft; and from an attentive examination, they difcovered it to be fpurious from the word *Parliament*, which, they prove, was not in ufe till near two hundred years after the Conqueft.—Sir Henry Spelman fays *, " Johannes Rex, haud dicam " Parliamentum, nam hoc nomen non " tum emicuit, fed communis concilii " regni, formam et coactionem perfpicuam " dedit."

And Prynne, in his animadverfions upon the 4th Inftitute of my Lord Coke, proves, that this word was not ufed in England till the time of Henry the Third.

But, after its introduction, it uniformly, for many centuries, fignified a Seffion of what we now call a Parliament.—In all the prorogations, from the firft records of Parliament, till at leaft the time of Henry the Seventh, the former Seffion is always called

* Gloff. Voc. *Parliamentum*.

called the laſt Parliament, or a Parliament held at ſuch a time and place. In the ſtatute of 4th Edward III. c. 14, which enacts, that a Parliament ſhould be held once every year, or oftener if need be, the word Parliament has always been conſtrued a Seſſion; for no one ever ſuppoſed there was any limit to the duration of Parliament, till the Triennial act, in the time of King William *. The firſt Parliament, after the convention, at the Reſtoration, ſat 17 years, and its length was never complained of as unconſtitutional. After the word *Seſſion* was introduced, and Parliament began to be applied to the duration of the writ of ſummons, ſtill the uſe of it was very unſteady and unſettled, as, in this very report, it has both ſignifications. When it is declared, that " buſineſſes in " one *Parliament,* or Seſſion of *Parliament,* " have been continued to the next S*ſſion* " of the ſame *Parliament,*" the firſt word *Parliament* can ſignify nothing but a Seſſion. Many other inſtances of this uncertainty, if it were neceſſary, might be adduced.

Hence

* 6 W and M. c. 2.

Hence we see the absurdity of that argument, which has been frequently used, *viz.* That, upon a writ of error, the *scire facias* is generally said to be returnable *ad proximum Parliamentum*, or the next Parliament. For the word Parliament, in this case, must necessarily signify the next Session, and not a Parliament, after a dissolution. For it would be the grossest folly to suppose, that the plaintiff in error might assign his errors in this Session, and have a *scire facias* to give notice to the defendant to appear in the next Parliament, which may now be after seven years, and might have been, we have seen formerly, after 17, or even 70 years.

* A learned friend of mine has suggested to me, in conversation, that the vulgar phrase, a *scire facias*, returnable in the next Parliament, though used in all times, is inaccurate, and, in fact, expresses a non-entity; that no *scire facias* could be sued out till the day

---

* I have since found, that this suggestion of my friend is confirmed by a MSS. of my Lord Hale's, who says expressly, that the *scire facias* must be returnable on a day certain.—P. 151.

day and place for the meeting of the next Seffion or Parliament were fixed, and that it muft be made returnable on a certain day; as far as I have been able to confider the nature of writs, and to examine the particular inftances, one of which is in the Regifter, p. 17, this obfervation is well founded.—Befides, it would be abfurd, and would defeat the purpofe of the writ, if the Sheriff might return at his pleafure the execution of the writ at any time, even upon the laft day of the next Seffion.— From whence it follows, that this writ cannot be fued out till after a prorogation or diffolution, and till the time of the next Seffion or Parliament is fixed by the King.

I have examined, with fome degree of attention, all the cafes of writs of error referred to by the report of 1673.

In thofe in the time of Ed. I. I can find nothing to lead me to declare whether they were pending after a prorogation or a diffolution

lution: but as there seems only to be a cessation of business during the holidays of Christmas, Easter, and Michaelmas, it affords some presumption that the vacations were only prorogations. But, upon examining the rest, with Prynne's catalogues before me, I find that three of those writs of error were proceeded on in new Parliaments: these are the cases in 1 R. II. 7 R. II. and 1 Hen. V. * The first is very remarkable, and proves that the record in a writ of error was not preserved in Parliament after a dissolution. The Earl of Salisbury is the plaintiff in error; he assigns his errors, and prays a *scire facias* to summon the defendant to appear in the next Parliament; and the Record proceeds—
" Et celle brief lui estoit grantez illoeques,
" & commandez estre fait retournable en
" dit proche Parlement: et puis après, sur
" *le fin du dit Parlement*, le dit Monsieur
" Johan de Cavendish, par comandement
" des Prelatz, & Seig'rs du Parlement, ent
" a lui fait portast mêmes les record & pro-
" ces

* Vide Appendix, v. and vii.

" ces en le Bank le Roi, pur y demurer,
" comme en garde, tan qu'au dit profch'
" Parlement; et eſt ordonnez et accordez,
" que mefmes les records et proces foient
" en dit profch' Parlement, par la caufe
" avant dite."

Here it is clearly ordered at the end of the Parliament, that the record and procefs fhould be carried back to the King's Bench, and that the whole fhould be brought up again in the new Parliament. In that of 7 R. II. n. 20, it is awarded only that the record and procefs fhall be in the next Parliament, and in that of 1. Hen. V. n. 19, the *fcire facias* only is awarded: though thefe two latter cafes are not fo full as the firſt, yet they are confiftent with it. But every authority of law concurred, that a writ of error was determined by a diffolution, till the order of the Lords in 1678; and from a confideration of the precedents which they produce, the Committee, in 1673, confine their report to prorogations, when they conclude that

" bufineſſes

" businesses depending in one Parliament,
" or Session of Parliament, have been con-
" tinued to the *next Session* of the *same* Par-
" liament; and whatever they had found in
point, in the case of a dissolution, they would
unquestionably have stated, because whatever proceeding would survive a dissolution,
would *à fortiori* survive a prorogation.

But the references to the Committee,
on the 11th of March and 17th of March,
1678, are extended to the effect of a dissolution; and the order of the House,
upon the report of this Committee, with
the cases which followed, would have
been conclusive and decisive at present,
that a dissolution did not disturb an Impeachment, if this order had not, a few
years afterwards, been reversed and annulled.

It is remarkable, that no precedent, authority, or principle whatever, is cited or
referred to by the Committee, for this precipitate and confident report.

But

But let us confider under what circumftances this order of the Houfe was made.

On the 5th of December preceding, Lord Stafford and four other Lords had been impeached for being concerned in the Popifh Plot; Lord Danby had been impeached alfo fome time afterwards in that month; and articles had been exhibited againft him by the Commons, charging him with high treafon. In January following, the Parliament was diffolved, and the new Parliament met again in March; and one cannot but fuppofe, that the Lords were infected with the madnefs of the times, or were ftruck with the general panic, when the Committee report within two days, and the Houfe order, without any precedent, or femblance of authority, that the impeachments were not affected by the previous diffolution.

But, in confequence of this order, the proceedings were continued in the next Parliaments againft Lord Danby and Lord Stafford

Stafford. The courſe of the proceedings againſt Lord Stafford was as fol lows:

* Anno 1678.
December 5, Impeached by the Commons.
December 28, Examined.

In the next Parliament, Anno 1679.
April 9, Heard his accuſation read.
April 26, Put his anſwer in.

In another Parliament, Anno 1680.
November 12, His trial appointed.
December 7, Condemned.

From whence it appears, that this Impeechment was pending in three different Parliaments. After he was pronounced guilty, he urged this in arreſt of judgment, and prayed that he might have counſel to argue it, which moſt unreaſonably and unjuſtly was denied him; ſo that the priſoner, who, from his fears, or the natural imbecillity of his mind, ſeems to have been in a ſtate of confuſion and ſtupidity during

* Vide Appendix.

during the whole of his trial, was left to suggest feebly to the Court, that there was no precedent to support the proceedings *.

Sir Francis Winnington, one of the Managers, replies, that at a conference between the two Houses in 1678, it had been settled to be the law of Parliament, upon a *search of precedents* in all ages (it would have been better if it had been a discovery or production of precedents from all ages).

Sir William Jones, another Manager, simply and candidly refers to the order of 1678. But Serjeant Maynard, a third, says, " that which is most insisted upon, is, that " this charge that is made against this Lord " was presented in another Parliament. It " is true; but under favour, what is once " upon record in Parliament may at any " time afterwards be proceeded upon.—It
" is

* Vide Harg. State Trials, 3 vol. p. 201. &c.—Mr. Hume says, he was selected as the first victim, from his age, infirmities, and narrow capacity. 8 vol. p. 139.

" is a *sudden objection*, but I conceive it hath been done.—However, in a case of this nature, where the life of the King, when our own lives, and our nation, and our religion lies at stake, if there were not, I hope you would make a precedent."

The learned Serjeant says it is a *sudden objection*; as if he had not been in parliament in the year 1678, and had never heard of it before. This proves how ill prepared the most learned men were at that time to support the order of 1678 by precedent or argument. We are told that this Gentleman was afterwards very active in bringing about the Revolution: if we knew nothing of him but what we see here, notwithstanding the solemnity with which he concludes, we should have reason to execrate his memory. That the Lords should make a precedent to deprive a Peer, or the meanest subject, whether innocent or guilty, of his life, but a Peer whom all the world now believe to have been innocent, is a propofition which every Englifhman muft fhudder at.

But Parliaments deferve little credit for the correctnefs of their proceedings, in times when the Houfe of Commons could contend that the King had no power to pardon a perfon impeached, and that the Bifhops had no right to vote upon any preliminary queftion, in capital cafes, in the High Court of Parliament. I fhall only obferve, upon thefe points, that no principle or authority can be found in which the King's prerogative to pardon (the equity of our criminal law) has ever been reftrained, but by the united concurrence of the Legiflature *.

It is true, that it does not extend to the barbarous and favage proceeding of appeal, which ftill remains a difgrace to the Eng- lifh

---

* The Rolls of Parliament abound with inftances of pardons, in cafes of impeachment. But now, by 12 and 13 W. III. c. 2. the King cannot pardon a perfon impeached before conviction.

lish Law; a prosecution which has not for its object the purposes of public justice, but the gratification of private revenge, that the misery and death of the criminal *sint solatio cognatis interemptorum*.

With regard to the other point, the Bishops retain their seat and voice in Parliament by a more ancient title than perhaps any of the Temporal Peers can produce at present, except the Duke of Norfolk, from his possession of the Castle of Arundel. The trifling quaint observation transmitted even by my Lord Coke, that they are not noble by blood, can signify nothing more than that their issue will not inherit their rank and dignity: so that to say a Bishop is not entitled to all the privileges of Peerage, because his blood is not noble, communicates no more intelligence to the mind, than to assert that a Bishop is not entitled, because he is a Bishop; for it will hardly be contended, that his Majesty cannot by his patent make a Peer for life, who should in every instance

stance be entitled to the rights of Nobility. And I should think that a doubt will never again be entertained, that the Bishops have every right and privilege of Peerage, which is consistent with the Canons of the Church, or which they have not voluntarily relinquished or lost by desuetude.

I make these short observations upon those important subjects, which I conceive are now well understood, in order to remark, that in times when such illegal and unconstitutional positions were advanced, and when the House of Commons, however animated with a spirit of liberty and justice, were unquestionably wrong in two grand points, there is a possibility, that even in conjunction with the Lords, they might be mistaken in a third; and that no great respect ought to be shewn to the resolutions of either House, when unsupported by principle or authority.

It appears that some of the Lords themselves considered the order of 1678 as an innovation;

innovation; even that very Lord Anglesea*, Lord Privy Seal, who afterwards was one of the three who protested against the reversal of it. He says it was *a great point gained to the Commons;*—but, when points are gained, points are lost; and, if either House of Parliament can gain a point, without an act of the Legislature, from the mischievous consequences of the precedent, many points may be lost to the Constitution and People of England.—The Commons certainly deny that they had gained a point; but, notwithstanding that, it is evident that it was Lord Anglesea's opinion that they had.

In 1682, Lord Danby moved the Court of King's-Bench, that he might be admitted to bail; and he argued his own cause with great learning and ability†: he asserted that the impeachment was at end by the dissolution; otherwise, as it was uncertain

---

* Vide Appendix.

† Vide his Speech, Harg. State Trials, Vol. 2, p. 746, and his case in the Appendix.

uncertain when another Parliament would be affembled, his imprifonment might be indefinite, or for life, which was repugnant to the fpirit of the Englifh Law and Conftitution. The Court declared that his arguments had great force, but that they muft remand him till the reft of the Judges were confulted upon a queftion of fuch magnitude. In February 1683, he and the other Lords were bailed to appear the firft day of the next Parliament, he having been in prifon near five years, and the other Lords more than that time.

No Parliament fat from 1681 till the 19th of May, 1685; upon which day, the firft and only Parliament of James II. affembled, when Lord Danby and the other four Lords appeared, agreeably to their recognifance, and prefented petitions ftating the circumftances of their refpective cafes, and prayed that the Lords would bring them to a fpeedy trial, or do whatever they might think juft: upon which, the queftion was put, on the 22d of May, Whether

Whether the Order of the 19th of March, 1678, shall be reversed and annulled as to Impeachments?—It was resolved in the affirmative, three Lords only protesting against it: and upon this, Lord Danby and the four Lords were discharged, with their sureties, from their recognisance. It must be observed, that there is another case, which happened after the Order of the 19th of March, 1678, and before its reversal; in which an Impeachment was continued after a dissolution; that is the case of Sir William Scroggs, Chief Justice of the King's-Bench: on the 7th of January, 1680, he was impeached, and articles were then exhibited. On the 18th, Parliament was dissolved; on the 21st of March, the new Parliament met; on the 24th of March, the answer of the Chief Justice was read; but nothing farther was done in it.*

It has generally been argued as if this vote

* Vide Appendix, the Report on the 25th of May, 1717. p. xxiv.

vote of 1685, and the difcharge of Lord Danby and the four other Lords in confequence of it, merely cancelled the order of 1678, and deftroyed the effect of the cafes fubfequent to it; fo that the Law upon the fubject ought to be confidered and collected, as if all thefe orders and cafes were expunged, or had never exifted. I cannot but think that this conceffion is more extenfive than is neceffary to grant; and that, when the order of 1678, and the fubfequent cafes, are fairly weighed againft the vote of 1685 and the proceedings in confequence, there is a confiderable balance in favour of the latter. I fhall not lay any ftrefs upon the general fury in 1678 againft the Roman Catholics, from an idle apprehenfion of univerfal deftruction: but it clearly appears, that the Lords came to the refolution, after an inquiry of two days only, that in confequence of this order one venerable Peer loft his life, and five others remained in prifon fix years with conftant apprehenfions of fharing the fame fate. From thefe circumftances, cumstances, the legality of the order in 1678 must have been perpetually under contemplation: when therefore the Lords came to the vote in 1685, they had the benefit of the mature confideration and reflection of the laft feven years. But, befides this difadvantage, the very terms and nature of the vote prove, beyond all controverfy, their real and fincere opinion of the order of 1678. I fhall now fuppofe, for a moment, that it was the only object of the Lords in 1685 to protect the impeached Peers in defiance of all law and precedents, and confequently were determined to remove every obftacle to their defign. If they had thought there had been any authorities in corroboration of the order of the year 1678, they would have refolved generally that Impeachments abated by a diffolution, which would have over-reached every principle and precedent to the contrary; but when they fimply refcind the order of 1678, they muft have been convinced that there was no further enemy to encounter, or that this folitary

order

order was unsupported by any allies or auxiliaries. If the order of 1678 had been merely declaratory of the former law, the reversal would have been ineffectual and nugatory.

But it is said that the Parliament in that year was very profligate and corrupt. I confess I know no reason why these aspersions should be thrown upon the House of Peers at that time; for, before the end of the year, they made such opposition to the measures of the King, that he was determined never to meet them again: and the Bishops, who are generally supposed not to be the least obsequious of the Lords, throughout the whole of this reign conducted themselves with extraordinary spirit and firmness. And it is chiefly to the exertions of this House of Lords that we are indebted for the blessings of the Revolution.

We hear nothing more of this Question till the 5th of April 1690; when an Order was made, that a Committee should inquire,

quire, "Whether Impeachments continue "from Parliament to Parliament;" but, on the 7th of July, 1690, the Parliament was prorogued, and no report had been made: but, on the 2d of October, 1690, the Parliament met, after the prorogation, when Lord Peterborough and Lord Salisbury, who had been impeached on the 26th of October, 1688, in a former Parliament, of high treason, presented petitions to the House of Lords, stating they had been prisoners in the Tower near two years, and prayed the House to take their case into consideration. On the 6th of October they are bailed; and on the same day a Committee is appointed to inspect and examine precedents, whether Impeachments continue in *statu quo* from Parliament to Parliament. On the 30th of October, the Lords Committees produce the cases in the Appendix; upon a consideration of which, by the House, Lord Peterborough and Lord Salisbury were discharged from their recognizances.

This

This is a moſt important precedent; for it is reſolved upon, after a full and ſolemn inveſtigation of all the preceding caſes; and it ought not to paſs unnoticed, that this Committee called in the aſſiſtance of one of the moſt learned antiquarians of the age, Mr. Pettyt, that champion for the antiquity and dignity of the Houſe of Commons, that *aſſerter of the ancient rights of the Commons of England,* who would have been in raptures, if he could have produced authorities to have extended their power and juriſdiction.*

---

* At the end of this Report of the Committee, it is ſtated that Mr. Pettyt's Clerk read three records to the Houſe, the dates and numbers of which are given, but no abridgment of them. — (Vide Appendix, p. xviii). That in the 15th Ed. III. is the caſe of the Archbiſhop of Canterbury, which has already been noticed. The Record, 4 Ed. III. No. 16, is given at length in Foſter's Fourth Diſcourſe, p. 387; from which it appears, that Thomas de Berkele was tried in full Parliament by a jury of Knights, for being concerned in the murder of Ed. II. of which charge the jury completely acquitted him; but, becauſe he had appointed thoſe perſons his ſervants who had murdered the King.

It has been said that there is another point in this case, upon which the Lords may have discharged Lord Salisbury and Lord Peterborough, and not because they thought the impeachment determined by the dissolution. It is true they had consulted the Judges upon the effect of an act of general pardon, who delivered their opinions, That if the said Earl's crimes and offences were committed before the 13th of February 1768, and not in Ireland, nor beyond the seas, they were pardoned by the said act.

Two things, I think, in this case, are clear:

1st, That they did not discharge these Lords upon this act of pardon.

2d, That they could not possibly in point of law.

They

he was committed till the next Parliament, to hear his judgment, &c.—This was in the 4th of Ed. III; there are no new writs in the 5th of Ed. III; so that, on the day of this trial, probably a long adjournment (perhaps over Christmas) had been expected. The third Record referred to, I have not been able to find in the Collection of the printed Records.

They certainly thought there was such a probability of their being pardoned, that they might mitigate the rigour of their imprisonment, or, as is said in Lord Danby's case, might lengthen their chain, by admitting them to bail. But afterwards most consistently they proceed to inquire whether they ought to retain them under bail, which is only a gentler species of imprisonment, or whether their prosecution was not wholly at an end by the dissolution. Was Mr. Petyt called in to assist them in finding cases of pardons? The protesting Lords speak incoherently of pardons; but what they alledge besides the precedents produced, proves incontestably that the whole of this most industrious and solemn investigation was confined to this question solely, viz. Whether impeachments were determined by a dissolution?

But it was impossible, in point of law, that the Lords could give the Earls the benefit of this act, and discharge them
without

without putting them upon their trial. The crime of which they were accused, viz. of being reconciled to the Church of Rome, might be, and most probably was committed, if committed at all, since the 13th of February 1688, or in parts abroad. These exceptions were such, whether the parties must plead the act specially, or might have the advantage of it from a provision in the act itself upon the general issue, that no Judge or Court whatever could take notice of it but upon a trial, or upon hearing what the prosecutor had to answer to it.

It is certainly true that Mr. Justice Foster takes no notice of the question respecting the effect of a dissolution: but he says, the only use which he makes of this case is, " that the Lords exercised a " right of judicature without a High " Steward ;" * which they indisputably did when they inquired into the effect of

a

---

* Vide an extract from Mr. Justice Foster. Appendix, xliv.

a diffolution, and in confequence of that inquiry difcharged the prifoners.

The next cafe is that of the Duke of Leeds in 1701.* This is reprefented as the laft decifion upon the fubject, and as that gigantic precedent which has fwallowed up all the reft. I confefs, when I firft faw it, I thought it fuch a pigmy that I had almoft paffed it over without obfervation: and notwithftanding all that I have heard of it, I am not inclined to think more highly of it at prefent than I did at the firft. In the Lords Journals of the 24th of June, 1701, we find this Order:——" The Houfe
" of Commons having impeached Thomas
" Duke of Leeds of high crimes and mif-
" demeanours, on the feven and twentieth
" of April 1695, and on the nine and
" twentieth of the faid April exhibited
" articles againft him, to which he an-
" fwered; but the Commons not profe-
" cuting,

* Vide Appendix, p. xxviii.—This Duke of Leeds is the fame Lord Danby, who has fo often been upon the ftage before.

"cuting, It is ordered, by the Lords Spi-
"ritual and Temporal in Parliament aſſem-
"bled, That the ſaid Impeachment and
"the Articles exhibited againſt him ſhall
"be, and they are hereby diſmiſſed."

The inactivity of the Commons for ſix years would afford a preſumption that they had acquieſced in the deciſion of 1790:—but we are told they were obliged to advertiſe for a witneſs; but from the length of time, it ſhould ſeem, with no degree of ſucceſs. But the argument drawn from this caſe is this, viz. That the Lords muſt necefſarily have thought the Impeachment continued beyond the diſſolution, and that it was not extinguiſhed by that event; or they would not have given themſelves the trouble of diſmiſſing it. This muſt be admitted to be a fair argument; but the force and effect of it will depend entirely upon circumſtances. There is not a ſingle word expreſſed upon the queſtion, in the Order; but after our declarations it is true that our actions are the next beſt witneſſes
of

of our thoughts. But when an action is produced as evidence of intention, the whole chain of previous actions from which that action originated, ought to be taken into confideration, or we fhall be apt to pronounce an erroneous verdict from its teftimony alone.

And if this difmiffion of the impeachment does not prove, in the Lords, an act of deliberation upon the effect of a diffolution, it proves nothing more than any other order in their journals.

In the beginning of May 1701, there was a plentiful harveft of impeachments. The Earl of Portland, Lord Somers, the Earl of Orford, and Lord Halifax, had all been impeached in the courfe of that feffion: the Duke of Leeds had been impeached above fix years before, and more than one diffolution muft have intervened.*

On the 5th of May 1701, the Lords appoint a Committee " to draw a meffage to be

---

* The Triennial Act paffed 6 W. and M.

"be sent to the Commons, to put them in
"mind of the Impeachments brought up
"by them against the Earl of Portland, the
"Earl of Orford, the Lord Somers, and
"the Lord Halifax:" and a message was sent
in consequence to the Commons, "to ac-
"quaint them, that they having, on the first
"day of April last, sent up to their Lord-
"ships an Impeachment against William,
"Earl of Portland, of high crimes and
"misdemeanors; and having also on the
"fifteenth day of the same month several-
"ly impeached John Lord Somers, Ed-
"ward Earl of Orford, and Charles Lord
"Halifax, of high crimes and misde-
"meanors; their Lordships think them-
"selves obliged to put them in mind, that
"as yet no particular articles have been
,, exhibited against the said Lords, which,
"after *Impeachments have been so long de-*
"*pending*, is due in justice to the persons
"concerned, and agreeable to the methods
"of Parliament in such cases." This produced from the Commons, on the 9th of
May, articles against Lord Orford. On the
15th

15th of May, the Lords send again the same message verbatim, only omitting Lord Orford. On the 19th of May, the Commons exhibited articles against Lord Somers. On the 21st of May, the Lords send again the same message, including only the Earl of Portland, and Lord Hallifax, but vary the conclusion, thus, " which, after *Impeachments have so long depended, is a hardship to the persons concerned,* and not agreeable to the usual methods and proceedings of Parliament." On the 30th of May they send again the same message verbatim. The Commons answer, " As to your Lordships' message, the Commons take it to be without precedent, and unparliamentary; they, as prosecutors, having a liberty to exhibit their Articles of Impeachment in any time, of which they, who are to prepare them, are the proper Judges: and therefore, for your Lordships to assert, they having not yet exhibited particular articles against William Earl of Portland, and Charles Lord Hallifax, is a hardship to

"them, and not agreeable to the usual me-
"thods and proceedings in Parliament in
"such cases, does, as they conceive, tend
"to the breach of that good correspon-
"dence betwixt the two Houses, which
"ought to be mutually preserved."

And in another answer, the Commons complain of the frequent repetition of these messages.—On the 2d of June, the Lords reply, and conclude thus: "The Lords hope the Commons, on their
"part, will be as careful not to do any
"thing that may tend to the interruption of
"good correspondence between the two
"Houses, as the Lords shall ever be on
"their part; and the best way to preserve
"that is, for neither of the two Houses to
"exceed those limits, which the law and
"custom of Parliament have already esta-
"blished."

The Commons afterwards exhibited articles against Lord Halifax; and the Lords, after that, remind them again of the Earl
of

of Portland's impeachment.—The reader will fee why I have given fo full a narrative of thefe proceedings; for in all thefe meffages, in which Lord Portland's name is fent to the Commons five times, the name of the Duke of Leeds is never once mentioned.

From the 5th of May till the 24th of June, there are daily meffages between the two Houfes relative to the Impeachments; and within that time there are the moft angry refolutions, which are to be found in the Journals of the two Houfes. Lord Haverfham, at a conference, told the Commons, "That their Lordfhips cannot but
" look upon it as a great hardfhip, that
" any fhould lie under long delays in im-
" peachments: perfons may be incapable,
" facts may be forgotten, evidences may
" be laid out of the way, witneffes may die,
" and many the like accidents may hap-
" pen; and proceeded to fay, that it was a
" demonftration to him, that the Com-
" mons thought the Lords impeached in-
"nocent."

' nocent.'—This, of courfe, they refented, and complained to the Houfe of Lords againft Lord Haverfham, for thefe fcandalous words.

But, when the Lords were bringing charges againft the Commons for the hardfhip in keeping impeachments fo long depending, none of which had depended three months, would they not have reminded them, and upbraided them with the impeachment of the Duke of Leeds, if they had not thought it was totally terminated and extinct? And, when they were at open war with the Commons, for two months delay, in the cafe of the reft of the Lords, would they not have infinuated that the Duke of Leeds had experienced fome degree of hardfhip for the fpace of fix years?

But the Commons were refolved not to profecute, and the Lords were refolved not to difmifs. Lord Orford and Lord Somers had been put to the bar; and no profecutors appearing, they were acquitted.

On the laſt day of the ſeſſion, the charge againſt Lord Haverſham, and the impeachments againſt Lord Portland and Lord Halifax, are diſmiſſed; and that of the Duke of Leeds, who had never appeared, or had been heard of for ſix years before, is added to the liſt. From this account of the caſe, is it poſſible, that any candid man can conſider the Duke of Leeds's Impeachment like that of the Earl of Portland's or Lord Halifax's? and will he not think it a ſtrong confirmation of Lord Peterborough's caſe; and that the Lords, from their zeal to reſiſt (and perhaps to inſult) the Houſe of Commons, added the Duke of Leeds to the liſt, merely that he might make a figure upon paper, though they were convinced, in fact, he was a perfect ſhadow and non-entity? And is it within the ſcope of human credulity to ſuppoſe, that this was a deliberate determination and an unanimous reſolution, that this was neceſſary to the abolition of the Impeachment of the Duke of Leeds, when they had given no previous notice to the

the Commons, which they had done repeatedly in every other cafe; and when, a few years before, they had declared, almoſt *una voce*, that a diſſolution determined an impeachment; and when, a few years afterwards, there was a moſt ſerious debate whether a prorogation had not the ſame effect?

The next and laſt time that this queſtion came into diſcuſſion, was in the year 1717. The Earl of Oxford and Mortimer had been impeached of high treaſon, and of high crimes and miſdemeanors, on the 9th of July, 1715, when he was committed. In September afterwards, he anſwered, and the Commons replied and joined iſſue. On the 26th of June, 1716, the Parliament was prorogued. On the 10th of February afterwards, the Parliament met after the prorogation, on which day the Earl of Oxford preſented a petition to the Houſe of Lords, praying their Lordſhips to take his caſe under conſideration, and that his impriſonment might not be indefinite;

indefinite: upon which it was ordered, that all the Lords fhould be a Committee, to fearch for and report fuch precedents as relate to the continuance of Impeachments from feffion to feffion, or from Parliament to Parliament.

On the 25th of May, 1717, they report as in the Appendix; and it is refolved by the Houfe, that the Impeachment of the Commons againft the Earl of Oxford was not determined by the intervening prorogation of the Parliament.

From the Lords Debates, it appears that the divifion upon this queftion was 87 to 45; fo that 45 Lords at that time were of opinion that an Impeachment abated by a prorogation. Ten Lords protefted againft the refolution; and the mode of reafoning, in the proteft of the diffentients, is a ftrong authority with regard to a diffolution.

" Diffen-

" Diffentient,

" Becaufe there feems to be no diffe-
" rence in Law between a prorogation
" and a diffolution of a Parliament, which,
" in conftant practice, have had the fame
" effect, as to determination, both of ju-
" dicial and legiflative proceedings; and
" confequently the vote may tend to
" weaken the refolution of this Houfe,
" May 22, 1685, which was founded
" upon the law and practice of Parlia-
" ment in all ages, without one precedent
" to the contrary, except in the cafes
" which happened after the Order made
" the 19th of March, 1678; and, in pur-
" fuance hereof, the Earl of Salifbury was
" difcharged in 1690."

It is manifeft, from this proteft, that it muft have been the decided and unanimous opinion of the Houfe of Lords, that it would have been determined by a diffolution; for it is here affumed, as a firft and uncontrovertible principle; and if the next ftep were true, viz. that there was no difference

ference between a prorogation and a diffolution, the conclusion of the diffentients would have been a strictly mathematical demonstration.

This argument has been greatly misunderstood, and therefore I must endeavour to make my meaning more intelligible. I assert, that it appears from this protest, that it is manifest, in the opinion of the dissenting Lords, that the rest admitted that a dissolution would determine an Impeachment; for they argue thus:—You admit, or it cannot be denied, that a dissolution determines it; but a prorogation is equivalent to a dissolution; *ergo* a prorogation determines it. I care not, whether the second step and the conclusion are right or wrong; but the argument incontestably proves, that the diffentients thought that none in their House could controvert the first step or major of their syllogism.

Though I were ignorant of every proposition of Euclid's Elements, or were convinced that every one of his conclusions was false; yet, if I saw that he began with asserting, that " things which are equal " to one and the same thing, are equal to " each other;" and that the whole of his geometry was built upon it; I should conclude that Euclid was convinced, that every man in his time, who had a clear understanding, assented to that simple proposition.—But, say the Gentlemen, who deny the inference drawn from this protest, it even proves our case; for we can make as good an argument as the dissentients. We say that it is decided, that a prorogation does not put an end to it; and your protest affirms there is no difference between a dissolution and a prorogation; *ergo*, a dissolution does not put an end to it: but they must remember, when the intermediate step was advanced, there were 87 to 45 against it; so it is near 2 to 1 against their conclusion.

I confess, that none of the cases produced by this Committee, appear to me to prove much, except the first, with respect

spect to the present inquiry: but Drake's* case, in my mind, is a very strong instance to shew the prevailing opinion of the House of Lords, in the year 1660; for, after his conviction, by his pleading guilty, the Lords must necessarily have thought that the Impeachment would be determined by the dissolution, and that they could not give judgment in the next Parliament without a fresh trial; for, if that had not been their opinion, it is highly probable they would have wished to have given judgment themselves; and besides, if it had not been at an end, I apprehend the Attorney-General cold not have prosecuted for the same offence, in the inferior Courts.

† Fitzharris, who, though a Commoner, was impeached by the House of Commons, in 1681, for high treason (another instance of the wild unconstitutional experiments of those times), was indicted, and pleaded to the indictment, that there was an impeachment pending against him for the same

---

* Vide Appendix, 25 May, 1717.
† Harg. State Trials, Vol. III. p. 226

same crime. This plea was over-ruled by the Court of Kings-Bench for defect in form. But as the Lords afterwards rejected the Impeachment of Fitzharris, the inferior Courts would now be justified in declaring such a plea bad, from the inefficacy or nullity of the Impeachment: but where a person is impeached, before the House of Lords, of crimes of which they legally and constitutionally have cognizance, the pendency of the Impeachment, I apprehend, might be pleaded in abatement to an indictment; otherwise this solecism would be the consequence, that a person might be punished in two different Courts for the same offence. I am aware that it has been held*, that the pendency of one indictment cannot be pleaded in abatement to another, for the same offence; but I should think that this must be confined to indictments in the same Court.

But, upon this subject, as I find nothing certain, I speak with diffidence: but it is surely

* R. v. Stratton Doug. 228. Hawk. c. 34. sect. 1. &c.

surely not unreasonable to suppose that the Lords thought their jurisdiction at an end, when they directed the Attorney-General to commence a fresh prosecution.

Peter Longueville* had been impeached, but was never prosecuted after the dissolution: but eight of his associates had been convicted, and heavily fined: so the Commons might reasonably think that preventive justice had been sufficiently satisfied.

It is remarkable, that Lord Stamford's seems to be the only case of an indictment which was not prosecuted with effect, in the same Parliament to which the indictment was sent; but, as it does not appear that he ever was arraigned, or pleaded to the indictment, I can hardly think that any inference can be drawn from it. I should suppose, that an indictment, properly found by an inquest of 12 men, can never discharge its office till it is quashed by an act of the court, or the party has pleaded to it. The words of the *certiorari* are,

* Vide Appendix, 25 May, 1717.

are, that "We * do command you (the Justices of Oyer and Terminer), that you do send, under your seals, before us, *in our present Parliament*, all and singular indictments, &c." Upon the return of this writ, the indictment must be in the custody of the Clerk or *custos rotulorum* of the House of Lords; and I should think that, without further *certiorari* or mandate, the next or any Parliament might proceed upon it, like a commissioner of goal-delivery, when the defendant is in custody, upon the Coroner's inquest, or an indictment found at Quarter-Sessions; and I should imagine, that there could be little doubt but the Clerk of Parliament might be directed, by *certiorari*, to send this indictment to the Court of the Lord High Steward.

I shall now consider some cases in the Courts of Law, which are supposed to be authorities upon this subject. I have given the

* Vide the case of the Dutchess of Kingston. Vol. XI. Harg. State Trials.

the cafe of Lord Danby at full length in the Appendix; but I do not fee what inference on either fide can be collected from it. The Court of King's Bench, it is agreed, have a difcretionary power of bailing, even in cafes of treafon or felony, perfons committed by the Houfe of Lords, when Parliament is not fitting; for circumftances may appear, which may render it a debt of juftice, that they fhould be liberated from confinement; and there would be a failure in the difcharge of that juftice, if fuch a power were not vefted in the Court of King's Bench. The next cafe is that of Lord Salifbury, who had been committed in a former Parliament upon an impeachment for high treafon: his imprifonment had been continued; and, upon an adjournment for two months, he applied to the Court of King's Bench, to be bailed. His counfel argued, that he ought to be bailed, becaufe he was entitled to the benefit of an act of pardon. The Court declared they could take no notice of that act, becaufe there were many exceptions in it.—And with respect to the other ground, the Court of King's Bench had never discharged any person committed by the Peers for treason or felony. And this question respecting the effect of a dissolution at that time, was certainly a doubtful point; as appears from the subsequent inquiry and determination in the House of Lords, in this very case of Lord Salisbury. And it was impossible for the Court of King's Bench to declare, that the Lords jurisdiction was at an end, when the proceedings in consequence of the order of 1678, had made it such a subject of debate and controversy. But whatever might have been the opinion of the Court, every person must think they acted with great propriety; as Lord Salisbury's imprisonment had been continued by the House after the dissolution, and as they had only adjourned for two months, when they remand his Lordship, and recommend him to make an application to those by whom he had been committed *.

The

* Vide Lord Salisbury's case at length, in the Appendix, p. xlii.

The next case is that of Peters and Benning, which was a question, whether a writ of error, under particular circumstances, abated by a dissolution; in which it is stated, that Lord Holt advanced that impeachments continued after a dissolution. From the internal evidence of the case, one would conclude, that Lord Holt must have said directly the reverse, and that the reporter must have omitted the negative particle. This may be thought an easy way of disposing of this extrajudicial dictum of my Lord Holt. But I appeal to the candid or to the most uncandid reader, if there is any consistency in this, viz. " And per
" Holt, If an impeachment be in one Par-
" liament, and some proceedings thereon,
" and then the Parliament is dissolved, and
" a new one called, there may be a conti-
" nuance upon the impeachment; and he
" quoted the case of James and Bertly,"
&c. in which a writ of error was determined by a prorogation.—And the whole tenor of this case is to prove that writs of error determine by a dissolution, and that,

in the year 1701, the Court of King's Bench were not bound by the extrajudicial order of the Lords in 1678. This incoherent and heterogeneous report is given at full length in the Appendix, p. xlvi.

Comyns's Digest has been cited, where this propofition is found, viz. " When a
" Parliament is diffolved, appeals or writs
" of error pending in Parliament do not
" abate by the diffolution, but the next
" Parliament fhall proceed upon them in
" the ftate which they were in at the dif-
" folution, without beginning *de novo*." Ray. 383*. " So an impeachment by the
" Commons is not altered by a diffolution." Ray. 383.

In Sir Thomas Raymond's Reports, to which Comyns refers, it is fhortly ftated, that Lord Stafford applied to the Court of King's Bench to be bailed; and Mr. Juftice Raymond fays, " we did not think fit, in
" difcretion, to bail him, and we alledged
" likewife

---

* Parliament, p. 2.

" likewife the orders of the Houfe of
" Lords, *though we did not rely thereon,*"
which are as followeth: and then the order
of 1678, &c. is ftated as in the Appendix.

So Comyns refers here to an author, who
fays the Court did not rely upon what they
alledged; and at beft, it is but an abridgment of the order of 1678. Chief Baron
Comyns's Digeft is a moft valuable dictionary; but as every dictionary of language
contains many words which no good writer
or perfon of delicacy would adopt, fo every
dictionary of law contains many propofitions which no experienced or judicious
lawyer would rely upon.—Lawyers would
make ftrange confufion in the affairs of
their clients, if they gave them advice from
Comyns's Digeft, though it is the beft book
extant of its fort. It is intended only to
facilitate labour, by directing us where we
may find more information upon the fubject; and our conclufions muft be drawn
from a comprehenfive and comparative view
of the authorities at length.

Chief Baron Comyns is always regarded as very high authority, when he gives his own opinion, and refers to no other book; but otherwife, his Digeſt is nothing but an alphabetical abridgment of the authors he has read, without taking any refponſibility upon himſelf. But it may be aſked, why does he not refer to the order of 1685? Becauſe it is clear, that he had never undertaken the arduous taſk of reading over the Journals of the Houſe of Commons and Houſe of Lords, with an intent to make an index or abridgment of them; and moſt probably we ſhould have had no abſtract of the order of 1678, if he had not found it in Sir Thomas Raymond's Reports; and even here, he makes no reference to the Lords Journals. But notwithſtanding this abridgement, in direct contradiction to it, two or three paragraphs afterwards, he tells us, that " a writ of error is determined by " a diſſolution, and there ſhall be another " writ of error at the next Parliament, " 2 Cro. 342." And in the preceding page, he informs us, " That all orders,
" and

" and *every thing before Parliament*, deter-
" mine by a prorogation, except a *scire
" facias* and a writ of error."

But in opposition to these fragments of cases, I might cite the authority of a very learned author, who professes to give you what he thinks, upon mature and profound deliberation, the best law upon every subject he investigates, and who did not intend his work merely as an assistant to students and practisers, but a rule of action for Judges and Magistrates; I mean, Mr. Serjeant Hawkins *. He says, " All the or-
" ders of Parliament are determined by a
" dissolution or prorogation; and *all mat-
" ters* before either House must be *com-
" menced anew at the next Parliament*, ex-
" cept only in the case of a writ of error."

In my opinion, all these cases and quotations prove exactly nothing at all; but, upon a general review of the Precedents, it appears that there never was a case in which the

* Bk. 2. c. 15. sect. 74.

the proceedings of an Impeachment were continued after a diffolution, before the Lords made the Order of the 19th of March, 1678; and that the cafes of Lord Stafford and the other four Popifh Lords, Lord Danby, and Sir William Scroggs, were legalized by no authority but that Order. The cafe of Lord Peterborough and Lord Salifbury was decided, after a full inveftigation and mature confideration of principles and precedents anterior to 1678, and from a conviction that the three fubfequent cafes had no legal and conftitutional foundation: the authority alfo of this precedent derives fuch ftrength from the proceedings in my Lord Oxford's cafe, as to bid defiance to every attack which induftry or ingenuity can make againft it *.

But

---

* I fay nothing here of the Duke of Leeds's cafe; though, from the account I have given of it, I fhould fuppofe that it will be thought rather to corroborate, than to weaken the authority of the decifion in 1690.

But I shall endeavour to prove that this case is strongly fortified both by ancient authorities, and by general principles.

I have already observed, that in our researches into the records of Parliament, we must be cautious in distinguishing, when we find the same person mentioned in different Parliaments, whether it is a continuation of the first proceeding, or whether in the subsequent Parliament it is not an original transaction. No one can be supposed to have read the rolls of Parliament from the beginning to the end; and therefore it is impossible to pronounce with certainty what does not exist, or may not be found there. But, among all the cases which I have examined, the Archbishop's arraignment is the only one, where there is a clear continuation of the same proceeding or prosecution. In all the rest which I have seen, where the name is repeated in a subsequent Parliament, a new and original proceeding is instituted. And from the time of Edward I.

to the reign of Henry VIII.* I have not seen one petition which was prefented in one Parliament, and anfwered in another; and through all the rolls of Parliament, till that time, every Impeachment is in the form of a Petition.

In the 50th of Edward III. feveral perfons had been impeached, and various judgments pronounced, according to the offence or prayer of the petition.

In the new Parliament, in the 51ft of Edward III. after the petitions of the Commons were read and anfwered, the Speaker of the Commons informed the King and the Lords, that feveral perfons had been impeached in the laft Parliament without due procefs, and adjudged to undergo various punifhments; and therefore he prayed, that in this Jubilee Year they might be reftored to their former eftate and degree, notwithftanding their judgments. The King afked

if

* The printed records of Parliament extend no farther.

if his requeſt extended to all who had been impeached; and having declared, to all, the King ordered the Commons to make a bill for each perſon, that he might extend his grace to which he pleaſed. Upon which ſeven petitions or bills are preſented, in moſt of which it is ſtated, that the perſon was impeached in the laſt Parliament wrongfully and of great malice, and the bill prays that he may be included in the pardon.—After theſe petitions, there is this remarkable memorandum:

Fait a remembrer que en ceſt Parlement nulle reſponce eſtoit faite par les ditz Seign'rs a les dites ſept Billes cy deſſus proſcheinement eſcritz, *ne poet eſtre a cauſe que le dit Parlement s'eſtoit departiz & finiz* a meſme le jour, devant que rienz ne fuſt pluis fait a ycelles. Here is a clear declaration that no anſwer can be given to a petition but in the Parliament in which it is preſented. Though theſe petitions are here called bills, yet they begin, like all the other petitions, with Prie le Commune, or les Communes priont, &c.

In

In the 7th of R. II. n. 3. this entry is made in the margin: "Responsio vacat, "quia sic non placuit Domino Regi *pro* "*tunc* illud concedere. Et *ideo* cancellatur "& damnatur."---This proves, that if parliamentary petitions were not anfwered in the fame Parliament, they were cancelled and void. In the 8th year of Henry V. (Rot. Parl. n. 16.) we find a very remarkable inftance, which proves, that the Commons thought this an eftablifhed part of the conftitution, and they feel great jealoufy and apprehenfions that an innovation might be introduced in confequence of an extraordinary circumftance. While Henry was in France, the Duke of Gloucefter was appointed his Lieutenant, and Guardian of the kingdom, and a Parliament had been fummoned by writs under the tefte of the Guardian. In this Parliament feveral of the petitions are anfwered, "Soit faite comme eft defiré, fi le pleft au Roi," and "Soit advifée par le Roi."

From

From thefe conditional anfwers the Commons faw that it might introduce the cuftom of anfwering petitions out of Parliament, or of refuming them in another Parliament; and therefore to prevent this innovation they prefent a petition, in which they ftate, that they are informed by feveral of the Lords, that their petitions prefented in this prefent Parliament were not to be engroffed before they are fent into France to the King for his royal affent: they therefore pray that it may be ordained in this *prefent* Parliament, that all the petitions prefented *in this prefent* Parliament may be anfwered within the kingdom of England during this *fame Parliament*; and if any petitions remain not anfwered, and not terminated during this *fame* Parliament, that they fhould be void, and of no effect; and that this ordinance may be obferved in every future Parliament.—Refponfio. Soit advifée par le Roi.*—Here the Commons pray that their own petitions, if they are not abfolutely

* This petition is fo deferving of attention, that I have given it verbatim in the Appendix, xlviii.

lutely concluded in the same Parliament, may never be resumed, but may be perfectly void. And it clearly appears from the former authorities, and from the nature of this case, that this is a petition for the preservation of the ancient law, and not for the introduction of any new regulation.— This answer seems to import the same as " Le Roi s'advisera," which has always been considered a negative. But as this ordinance was intended to prevent, and not to produce an alteration, of course the law and usage of Parliament remained as it was before.

I have not observed more than one prorogation recorded in the Rolls of Parliament, before the time of Henry the VIth; but from the beginning of his reign, till the end of the reign of Henry the VIIth, there is a prorogation recorded in almost every Parliament, in Latin; except in the 2d of Henry VI. it is in French.

But

But what is most extraordinary, and what is a "confirmation strong as proofs of holy writ," of this doctrine, that impeachments and all business in Parliament end with a dissolution: in every prorogation, one reason assigned for the prorogation is, that the businesses before Parliament, on account of their *arduousness, cannot be discussed and finally terminated*, before Christmas, or some other time, when it becomes necessary for the Members to return home; therefore the King prorogues them to a future day, when they shall re-assemble, for the *final conclusion and determination* of the said businesses.

For what possible purpose can this reason be assigned for a prorogation, but because every business must be recommenced after a dissolution. It might be conjectured, perhaps, that this was done to save time, as they might be prorogued to a day before which they could not be convened after a dissolution; as, by the Magna Charta of King John, it was provided,

there

there should be 40 days between the teste and the return of the writ of summons. But that reason fails, as in most instances they are prorogued for more than 40 days; sometimes for two or three days more or less than 40; but often for two, three, or four months. In the first case which I have met with, 21 R. II. c. 36. this reason is assigned thus:—The King, considering that great causes and matters moved and pending in this Parliament, could not be terminated at that time, and for other reasons, adjourned the Parliament. Sometimes thus:—" Quod diversis petitionibus
" in eodem Parliamento exhibitis, minime
" responsum fuerit, nec adtunc commode
" fieri potuerit, Rex, &c. dictum Parlia-
" mentum prorogavit." 31 Hen. VI. n. 20. But in general, with very little variation of expression, the Chancellor declares: " qua-
" liter negotia Parliamenti, propter ipso-
" rum negotiorum arduitatem discuti non
" poterant nec finaliter terminari, Dominus
" Rex presens Parliamentum duxit pro-
" rogandum, et prorogavit to a time and
" place,

" place, when and where, pro finali con-
" clufione negotiorum Parliamenti predicti
" convenirent." That there may be no doubt that a prorogation was preferred to a diffolution, to prevent the deftructive effects of the latter; in three inftances, at the leaft, it is exprefsly declared :—" qualiter
" negotia per Communes, *ante diffolutionem*
" *ejufdem Parliamenti providend' ordinand'*
" *& notificand'* adoptata, difcuti non pote-
" rant, nec finaliter terminari," the Parliament is prorogued. 8 Hen. VI. n. 16; 27 Hen. VI. n. 10; 12 & 13 E. IV. n. 11.

There is generally a reafon affigned, why the Parliament fhould be difmiffed, as that the Noblemen might have leifure to enjoy their recreations, and the Commons, " circa congregationem frugum," to collect their crops; or on account of the approach of Chriftmas or Eafter, &c. but the reafon why they are difmiffed by a prorogation, and not by a diffolution, is always this, that bufinefs is unfinifhed.

In one case, a particular business unfinished is specified; the record of which prorogation I have given at length in the Appendix, p. xlix.

The reader will now see what strong ground I had to intimate, that it was probable that the Parliament might be prorogued and not dissolved, on account of the pendency of the arraignment of the Archbishop of Canterbury. But no distinction which I have been able to discover, in the Rolls of Parliament, is made in the *petitio & negotium* of an impeachment; and the other *negotia & petitiones* before Parliament; and it will be incumbent upon those who maintain that an impeachment can survive a dissolution, to point out when and how that distinction originated. My Lord Coke cites his manuscript,—Modus tenendi Parliamentum, &c. which declares " The Parliament ought not to be ended, " while any petition dependeth undiscussed,
" or

" or at the leaft, to which a determinate
" anfwer is not made."*

† Prynne, with his accuftomed hoftility to this manufcript, declares, " that though
" this is an ufual, it is no general binding
" law or cuftom; many Parliaments having
" been ended before all petitions in them
" have been anfwered; yea, certain Lords
" and other Commiffioners, or the King's
" Council, have been appointed to anfwer
" after Parliaments ended; and refers to
" various inftances:" but in all thofe inftances, thefe Commiffioners were appointed by the authority of Parliament itfelf.

After thefe authorities, we fhould be a little furprifed, if the proceedings in the Duke of Suffolk's cafe, in the 28th year of Hen. VI. were a contradiction to them.—
But,

---

* 4 Inft. 11.
† Prynne's Animadv. 15.

But, upon a minute examination of that case, I find, in every instance, it is strictly conformable to this general doctrine.

In the 28th year of Hen. VI. * the Commons, by their Speaker, *accusaverunt et impetiti fuerunt Willielmum De la Pole Ducem de Suffolk, de quibusdam proditionibus, &c. prout in quadam* BILLA *certos articulos continente magis evidenter apparebit*: and they beseech,—*ut dicta billa in præsenti Parliamento inactitaretur*; and that it might be proceeded against the Duke *in eodem Parliamento*, according to the law and custom of England.—And after stating the articles, they conclude,—" And of all the treasons in these articles " contained, we accuse and *empeche* the said " Duke of Suffolk,—and pray, that this " be *enact*, in this your High Court of " Parliament, and thereupon to proceed, " in this your *present Parliament*, as the " matters aforesaid require, &c."

They

* N. 18.

They afterwards prefer additional articles, which they conclude as before.—The Duke anfwered the articles, but did not afterwards put himfelf upon his *Parage*, but fubmitted himfelf to the King's *rule & gouvernaunce*. And the King ordered him to be banifhed the kingdom for five years; upon which feveral of the Lords requefted to enter a proteft, that this was not done by their advice and concurrence, and that it might not afterwards be confidered as a precedent.

In the next year, the 29th of Henry VI. a new Parliament after a diffolution was fummoned. The new Commons were diffatisfied with the proceedings of the King with refpect to the Duke of Suffolk in the laft Parliament. But they do not demand that he fhould be put upon his Peerage, according to the articles of impeachment exhibited in the former Parliament, and that he fhould be proceeded againft according to the law and cuftom of Parliament, and that a proper judgment fhould be pronounced upon

upon that impeachment; but they carry up a petition, in which they state at length all the former articles, and the procefs thereon, and requeft that it may be granted, ordained, and eftablifhed, that the faid Duke fhould be deemed and declared a traitor. The King anfwers, " Le Roi s'advifera."*

This is clearly a bill of attainder, and as much a new and original proceeding as Lord Strafford's bill of attainder was feparate and diftinct from his impeachment.—So far I wifhed to confider this cafe upon the authority of the records of Parliament folely; but if we can give credit to the chroniclers of the times, this could not poffibly be a continuation of the impeachment: for at this time the Duke had not only been banifhed, but had been beheaded; and this confequently muft have been a bill of attainder after his death.

Moft

* I have given the firft part of this petition or bill verbatim in the Appendix, p. 1.; the remainder only ftates at large the confequences of the attainder—as forfeiture, corruption of blood, &c.

Most of my readers will remember the Duke of Suffolk and Captain Whitmore, in Shakespeare's Henry the VIth.

But I shall now examine how far the decision of 1690, and these ancient authorities, are supported by general principles.

Impeachment is a kind of criminal prosecution, which modern times have reduced to system and consistency. It is certainly *sui generis*, and in many great points dissimilar and unanalogous to every other species of criminal procedure. The House of Commons, when they impeach, have been denominated, by high authority, the * *solemn Grand Inquest of the Nation* ; but this must be regarded rather as a compliment to exalt their dignity, than an assertion that, in reality, they exercise the function of a Grand Jury, and are to be governed by the same rules. If we pursue the allegory (and in truth it is nothing more), we should degrade the Lords to the less dignified character of the *Petty Jury of the Nation*.

With the same propriety, the Attorney-General, who *ex officio* can file an information for a misdemeanour committed in any part of England, upon which the defendant may be tried, without the intervention of a Grand Jury, might be called a Grand Inquest of the Nation. The Commons, in one case, like the Attorney-General in the other, are, in every stage of the proceeding, merely prosecutors; but, as they prosecute in the name of themselves and all the Commons of Great-Britain, they need not require a more honourable appellation.

When they inquire whether there are grounds to impeach, they do nothing more than what is done by every conscientious prosecutor, who, with scrupulous caution, will convince himself that there is a just reason, or *probable cause*, to prefer the accusation; and both from principles of justice, and the current of authorities, the House of Commons are bound to admit the party to go as far into his defence as he may think proper, or be advised.

But

But though the House of Commons are the prosecutors who have joined issue with the defendant in an impeachment, I should think it but a puerile argument, that the impeachment is at an end by the extinction of that House, as an action or an appeal abates by the death of the plaintiff. *All the Commons of Great Britain,* whether the expression may be taken in the ancient sense of the *electors,* or in the modern vulgar acceptation of *the people at large,* may be presumed, like the King,* never to die; but, as the new House of Commons, and the new Managers, may be supposed to be perfect strangers to the party, and to the progress of the suit, one would be apt to suspect that the prosecution would be an unconnected and incoherent performance, unless the new House adopted the same means to obtain information as the preceding House; that is, by an

original

* Though, if one be indicted in the time of one King, and plead to issue, and afterwards the King dies, he shall plead *de novo.* 7 Co. 31. but now *contra,* by 1 Ann. c. 8.

original inquiry: and how is it poffible that thefe ftrangers can be convinced of the juftice and propriety of the continuation of the trial, but by an examination of the whole Houfe, or a report from their Committees, or, in fhort, but by the fame means by which the juftice and propriety of its commencement at firft were manifefted?

Whatever is true when part of the Houfe is changed, will alfo be true if the whole were changed. The Members of the Houfe of Commons have a right to infpect the Journals of the Houfe of Lords; but that is a right which will not affift them upon this occafion; for the evidence upon trials before the High Court of Parliament is never recorded. The Lords, upon the prefent trial, have ordered it to be taken down by clerks, and afterwards to be printed for their own benefit. But they were not bound to make fuch an order; nor can the Houfe of Commons claim any advantage from that circumftance; and therefore it
is

is possible that a new House of Commons may know nothing more, and have no better means of procuring information, of the progress of an impeachment unfinished in a former Parliament, than they would have of being acquainted with the circumstances of a trial conducted before the Court of Session in Scotland. If it should be alledged, that the former Managers might inform the new House by affidavits, I can only say that the Constitution has provided no power to compel such affidavits, or to give authenticity to them; for even if they were sworn before the Chancellor and the House of Lords, they would only be waste paper, and have no more validity than a common letter; nor is there any power to compel the former Managers to undergo an examination *vivâ voce* at the bar of the House. But this certainly is only an argument *ab inconvenienti* or *ex absurdo*.

When we look back to ancient times, we behold much confusion and obscurity; but yet there are certain objects which antiquarians can distinctly delineate: in general they agree, that when the Commons, or a certain number of the minor Barons, or free tenants of the Crown, were compelled by the King to attend the High Court of Parliament (a duty from which they had before been exempted, and a right which they seldom had had an inclination to assert), being too numerous, or too diffident, to sit in the same House with the Lords or greater Barons, they became humble petitioners to the King and to the Lords, to redress the grievances with which they and the country were oppressed*. Their petitions, either by stating general complaints, contained a prayer to provide measures to prevent, or, by describing particular offenders, a request to punish and correct; and the grant of the petition with *Soit droit fait comme il est desiré*, or *Le Roi le veut*, became the judgment of the Court, or the law of the land.

The

---

* *Les Communes prient à nostre Seigneur Roi, & à son Conseil, &c.* in the old Statutes and Records, *passim*.

The one species of petitions was the origin of Impeachments; the other, of Acts of Parliament. These are coëval, and so nearly related to each other, that they still bear a striking resemblance. Selden, in his Judicature of Parliament, says, that in ancient times the King expressed his assent to the judgment in an Impeachment for treason or felony. The conviction had then the declared concurrence of the Three Estates of the Legislature.* In treason and felony, the judgment is defined by the Law; but that judgment, as in other Courts, cannot be pronounced by the Lords till it is demanded by the Commons; and therefore, as they possess this transcendent power of pardoning immediately after the verdict, it would be injustice to the party, if the Commons were not acquainted with those circumstances which might recommend him to that

* In all the old authorities, it is the King and the Three Estates: but I know no use in separating the Lords Spiritual from the Lords Temporal; it simplifies both the ideas and expression to call the King, Lords, and Commons, *the three Estates.*

that benefit. In other cafes, the extent of the judgment within certain limits is in the difcretion of the Court; but it muft be previoufly demanded by the Commons. This feems to have been well underftood between the two Houfes fo long ago as the 1ft Hen. IV,* when the Commons declare that the judgments of Parliament appertain folely to the King and to the Lords; and the King replies: "Mefmes les Com-
"munes font *petitioners & demandours,* &
"que le Roi & les Seigneurs de tout temps
"ont eues, & averont de droit les juge-
"ments en Parlement en manere come
"mefmes les Communes ount monftrez."
So, though the judgment is pronounced by the Lords, the Commons are *demandours;* and if the execution of it is not arrefted by the pardon of the King, it ftill has the affent of the three Eftates of the Legiflature, or fupreme power of the Nation.

The Impeachment of a Commoner frequently contains a confiderable portion of

* Rot. Parl. p. 79.

of legiflation; and it is generally underſtood, that the two Houſes of Parliament may create both a crime and juriſdiction unknown to the Common Law, as adminiſtered by the inferior Courts;* for, till the 13th of Geo. III. c. 63†, no offences what-

* The Houſe of Lords, in Fitzharris's caſe, rejected the Impeachment for treaſon, in conformity with the declaration of the Barons, in the caſe of Simon Bereford, 4 Ed. III. 4 Bl. Com. p. 259; becauſe he was not their peer, and other Courts were competent to bring him to juſtice: but they have never declared that they will not receive an Impeachment for a miſdemeanor cognizable in the inferior Courts by indictment or information. Indeed, there ſeem to be ſeveral caſes to the contrary. Drake's caſe clearly proves that the libel was ſuch, that the Lords thought that the Attorney-General might proſecute: Dr. Sacheverell, I apprehend, might alſo have been proceeded againſt by indictment or information. This difference of conduct in caſes of felony and miſdemeanor, is not, I think, eaſy to reconcile.

† This act contains a ſection which provides, that, when the Chancellor, or Speaker of the Houſe of Commons, ſhall ſend to India for evidence, no bill, or other proceeding depending in Parliament, ſhall be determined by a prorogation or diſſolution,

whatever, except murder, committed in India, were cognizable in the ordinary Courts of Juftice in England; but, if any atrocious or ruinous act had been committed there by a Britifh fubject, the perpetrator, I conceive, might, in all times, have been compelled to anfwer for it as a *high crime and mifdemeanor*, in an Impeachment before Parliament.

I premife this parity in the origin, and fimilarity in the exercife, of the legiflature and judicature of Parliament, to fuggeft, that, in doubtful cafes, we may fairly draw an inference from the one to the other, and conclude, that if the two Houfes, after a diffolution, have not power to complete an imperfect Act of Parliament, they have not jurifdiction to continue an unfinifhed Impeachment.

This till the evidence arrives; but the claufe is drawn with great caution, to prevent Parliament from expreffing any opinion relative to an Impeachment. So, from this act, no argument can be raifed.

This may be thought to prove nothing, by proving too much, as it would make Impeachments either determine by a prorogation, or an unfinished statute continue in *statu quo* after a prorogation. There can be little doubt but this used to be the case with public statutes; and it is only altered by a resolution of each House not to assent before the King to a bill which had not passed the other House in the same session. And, that the House of Commons may not be surprised when the King convenes the two Houses in full Parliament, the Lords always previously send a message to the Commons, to inform them that a bill sent from them has passed through the ceremonies of their House; and it afterwards receives the joint assent in the Assembly of all the Estates. That the King could have given his assent to a bill passed the two Houses any number of sessions before, provided it was in the same Parliament, is clear from Brooks's Abridgment,* where this is laid down:

O " If

---

* Title Parlement, pl. 86, 33 Hen. VIII.

"If there be divers feffions in one Par-
"liament, and the *King figns not a bill till
"*the laft,* then all is but one and the fame
"day, and all fhall have relation to the
"firft day of the firft feffion; and the firft
"day and the laft are but one Parliament,
"and one and the fame day, unlefs fpecial
"mention be made in the act when it
"fhall take its force: but every feffion
"wherein the King figns bills is a day by
"itfelf, and one *Parliament* by itfelf, and
"fhall have no other relation but to the
"fame feffion."

But fo late as the 38th Hen. VI* we find an impeachment anfwered by the King precifely in the fame words by which he gives his negative to a public ftatute.

The Commons impeach Lord Stanley for not bringing his tenants to fupport the King, and becaufe his brother had joined the Earl of Salifbury at the battle of Bloreheath. The Impeachment begins thus:
"To

* N. 38.

" To the Kyng our Soveraigne Lord.
" Shewen the Commons in this prefent
" Parliament affembled;" and then it ftates
the articles, and concludes : " Of all which
" matters doon and commytted by the faid
" Lord Stanley, we youre faid Commons
" accufe and empeche hym, and pray your
" mooft high Regalie that the fame Lord
" be commytted to prifon, there to abide
" after the fourme of lawe."—To which
the King immediately anfwers, *Le Roi s'ad-vifera.*

Some gentlemen have thought that perhaps the record may remain in force, like the record of an indictment, or of an inqueft; but they will fee that it has never been treated as fuch, except between the years 1678 and 1685 : but it has always been confidered a parliamentary record, or like the record of a ftatute, which, unlefs determined in the fame Parliament, acording to the words cited before, *cancellatur & damnatur.*

But

But the great principle upon which all proceedings depending in Parliament are or were determined by a diffolution, is this, viz. that the writ or commiffion by which the Court fat and exercifed jurifdiction, is at an end. It cannot but be obferved with what reluctance the two Houfes of Parliament acknowledge any kindred or connection with the inferior Courts. They confider it an humiliating circumftance to have any principle in common with a quarter-feffions: but there are certain principles which pervade the whole fyftem of law, like certain principles in nature which extend throughout the univerfe. It is no diminution to the fplendor of a diamond, that it owes its weight to that principle which gives a proportionate degree of gravity to a pebble; and we are told that the father of our philofophy, by obferving that an apple was drawn to the earth, juftly concluded that, by the fame principle, the plants muft be drawn towards the fun. But as it is generally fuppofed that the Courts at Weftminfter were originally

only

only committees from the Aula Regis, or the High Court of Parliament, the two Houses need not be ashamed if they find there preserved entire those principles, which were at first derived from themselves. The Barons of the Exchequer still retain their primæval title. It has been a common observation in every company, that, as the House of Lords is a Court of Record, their proceedings must continue in *statu quo*, like the proceedings of the Courts at Westminster, and the Court of Quarter-Sessions.

I am inclined to think, too, that the continuation of the proceedings in all Courts ought to be precisely the same, unless a satisfactory reason can be assigned for the difference; and, by the Common Law, I apprehend, the High Court of Parliament, the Courts at Westminster, the Court of Quarter-Sessions, and perhaps all other Courts, were subject to the same rules, with regard to the commencement and termination of their jurisdiction: but

several

several Acts of Parliament have made regulations in the Courts of Westminster and Quarter-Sessions, which have not extended to the Court of Parliament itself.

It is a general principle in the English Law, that the King is the fountain of all jurisdiction, and that all Judges derive their authority from him by commission or writ; which words are frequently, upon this subject, synonymous*: and it is also another general principle, that, upon a revocation or dissolution of that commission, all causes and proceedings before the Judges appointed by it, were determined, and must be commenced *de novo* before their successors. This latter principle seems to be grounded upon a fundamental rule of justice, that no Judge shall condemn whom he has not heard, or whom he has but partially heard; and the proceedings before his predecessor must, with respect to him, be considered *coram non judice*. Upon the death of the King, all commissions were dis-

* 2 Hawk. 20.

dissolved; and consequently, all writs and causes pending before the commissioners abated, and must have been instituted afresh. Chief Baron Comyns says, " At " Common Law, all actions abated by the " demise of the King, and the defendant " went without day."* Much learning upon this subject, may be seen in the first chapters of 2 Hawkins's Pleas of the Crown; 7 Coke's Reports 30, where there is a chapter upon the discontinuance of process, by the death of Queen Elizabeth; and the statute of 1 Ed. VI, c. 7, which, by its provision for the future, will give the reader a perfect idea of the effect of the dissolution of a commission, in the inferior Courts, by the Common Law. By virtue of commissions from the King, the Judges of the different Benches at Westminster

* And therefore discharged. These are Chief Baron Comyns's own words. Com. Dig. Abatement, H. 38. It is remarkable that all judgments of acquittal do not say the defendant is innocent, or discharged, but *quod eat sine die,* or shall go without a day; *i. e.* any further time fixed for his re-appearance in Court.

minster, and the Justices of the Peace, exercise their authority. The Terms at Westminster, and Quarter-Sessions in the country, are only prescriptive or statutable times, from which and to which they continue and adjourn their jurisdiction; but, whenever their commissions expired, all causes before them were determined. By the Common Law, a new commission of the peace was a *supersedeas* to, or a dissolution of, the former commission, and all businesses pending before the Justices must have been at end; for it is expresly provided, by 1 Ed. VI. c. 7, that no process shall be discontinued by the grant of a new commission.* The same is also provided with respect to several other commmissions.

In consequence of several acts of parliament, intended to secure the independence of the Judges, and the permanence of their proceedings, the commissions of the four Judges of any one Bench

can

* See also 11 Hen. VI, c. 6.

can hardly ever be annulled at once, and the act of any one of them is effectual†; but, if all the Judges, for instance, of the Court of King's-Bench, should die before a new patent was granted, I apprehend, that all actions and prosecutions would be as much determined as they were by the demise of the King, before 1 Ed. VI. c. 7. Commissioners of Oyer and Terminer must both hear and determine the whole of a prosecution before them; and consequently the Commissioners, under one commission, can have no cognizance whatever of what passed under those appointed by a former commission. Commissioners of Gaol-Delivery can try a prisoner upon the Coroner's Inquest, or upon an Indictment found by the Grand Jury at the Quarter-Sessions; but, by the Common Law, if a prisoner had been tried by a Commissioner of Gaol-Delivery, and had been found guilty by the jury, but no sentence had been passed upon him, the next Commissioner of Gaol-delivery had no authority to pronounce

* 2 Hawk. 3.

nounce judgment; and, if he had been put again upon his trial, he might, it seems, have pleaded *autrefoits convict*; for the
" plea * of *autrefoits convict*, or a former
" conviction for the same identical crime,
" though no judgment was ever given, or
" perhaps will be (being suspended by the
" benefit of clergy, or other causes,) is a
" good plea in bar to an indictment; and
" this depends upon this principle—that
" no man ought to be twice brought in
" danger of his life for one and the same
" crime."

Therefore, when a felon had been convicted by a verdict, if the Judge had neglected to pronounce judgment upon him before his commission expired, the convict must afterwards have been discharged, for he could neither be sentenced nor re-tried by another Judge; and therefore, to provide against this case (probably some remarkable instance had occurred), it is expresly

* 4 Bl. Com. 336.

prefsly enacted by 1 Ed. VI. c. vii, f. 5, "that the Justices of Gaol-Delivery shall "have full power and authority to give "judgment of death against such person "so found guilty:" and My Lord Coke says, "Before this act, at the Common "Law, if a man had been indicted and "convicted by verdict or confession, before "any Commissioners, and, before judg- "ment, the King died, in that case no "judgment could have been given; for "the King, for whom the judgment "should have been given, was dead; and "the *authority of the Judges who should* "*give judgment, was determined*; and this "act doth remedy those special cases.*"

The reader's mind cannot but anticipate the application of these general and exten- five principles to the writ, or commission, by virtue of which the High Court of Parliament is constituted. When the King has

---

* 7 Co. 30.

has ordered * *quoddam parliamentum nostrum teneri*, or, *a certain Parliament to be holden*, each Peer has a right *ex debito justitiæ* to a writ of summons; but he has no inherent legislative, or judicial capacity annexed to his person; and till he has received his writ of summons, or commission, he has no right either to a voice or seat in Parliament: to this commission, he owes his authority; and that power which can create, can at any time destroy; so the jurisdiction of the Lords, like the jurisdiction of all Judges and Justices by the Common Law, can, at any time, be determined by the act, or the death of the King†; and before the triennial act, like all other commissions by the common law, it had no other limit. From the hereditary right of each Lord to a writ of summons when a Parliament is convened, many imagine that it must be an hereditary, or rather

an

* These have been the words, in all times, both in the Lords' writs and Commons' writs.

† By 6 Ann. c. 7. continued six months afterwards.

an eternal court. But from this it would follow, that they might be a court independent of the Commons, or independent of any commiffion. This is a right which may be waved, and an obligation which may be difpenfed with. And no Lord can exercife any judicial or legiflative act but when he is poffeffed of his commiffion, or writ of fummons. It is no argument, to fay that their proceedings ought to continue in *flatu quo,* becaufe they are the fame perfons; for the fame Judges might, upon a vacancy of their commiffions, have been re-appointed to the fame bench: yet we have feen, by the Common Law, every caufe muft have been re-heard.

And, in fact, the prefent Houfe of Lords may confift of entirely different members from the next Houfe of Lords; for, one half might either not infift upon having their writs of fummons, or might be excufed their attendance in one Parliament, and the other half in another.

With regard to the probable change among the Scotch Peers, no argument can be drawn from that circumstance, because, whatever was the law upon the subject, before the year 1707, it was not intended to be altered by the Act of Union with Scotland.

If the question was nearly *in equilibrio*, perhaps the convenience or inconvenience of present circumstances, might cause one side or the other to preponderate.

From these principles, we see the difference of the effect of a prorogation and dissolution; for, after a prorogation, the Lords and Parliament still sit under the same commission, and a prorogation is exactly similar to an adjournment from term to term, and from quarter-sessions to quarter-sessions*.

The

---

* 1 Lord Raymond, 343. Treby, Chief Justice, and the Court, declare, that the principal of the Parliament is the King; and when he comes to meet

The diffolution of Parliament imports the fame as the diffolution of every other Court, by the abrogation of the commiffion. We have feen before, from an authority out of Brook, that a Seffion of Parliament is, in law, confidered all one day. So the term at Weftminfter, from the beginning to the end, is all reckoned but one day.

Hence alfo, we may form a reafonable conjecture, how the words "Le Roi s'avifera" came to imply a negative, which are precifely the fame in their primary fignification, as the words which have been always ufed by all the Courts at Weftminfter, when they took time to confider of their decifion,

meet the two Houfes, then the Parliament begins. And this refembles the holding of other Courts, viz. when the Judges come, the Court is faid to be held. The adjournment of the Houfes is the act of each Houfe: but when the Parliament is adjourned by the King, they call it a prorogation. Heretofore adjournments and prorogations were looked upon as the fame thing, but the effects of them are very different at this day.

decision, viz. *curia advisare vult.*—*Le Roi s'advisera* import nothing more; and it is probable, that originally they only became an absolute negative, when the King had deprived himself of the power of assenting, by annihilating the Court and all its unfinished proceedings.

It is true, that writs of error, and the Scotch and other appeals, now remain in *statu quo,* after a dissolution; but I conceive this practice has no other foundation, but the extraordinary Order of the 19th of March, 1678, which was only *reversed and annulled as to Impeachments;* for, in the case of Heydon v. Godsalve, Cro. Jac. 342. Croke says expressly, that the " Court all " held (of whom Lord Coke was one), that " a writ of error in Parliament is, by the " dissolution of the Parliament, deter- " mined."*

Before

---

* Lord Hale says, If the Parliament be dissolved before judgment affirmed or reversed, then the writ of error is wholly discontinued and abated. MSS. p. 167.

Before the Lords made this order in 1678, every Writer, Lawyer, Judge, Commoner, and Peer, concurred, without a single diffenting voice, that a writ of error was determined by a diffolution of Parliament.

It is faid, that there is a principle eftablifhed in this order of 1678, refpecting writs of error, which may now be extended to any other fpecies of judicial proceeding. The only principle I can difcover in it, is that of encroachment and ufurpation ; and becaufe you have done one uncontrovertible and flagrant act of ufurpation, you may fafely venture to do another.

But had the order of 1678 been as confonant, as it is manifeftly repugnant, to every authority with regard to writs of error, I fhould hardly think that any conclufion can be drawn, applicable to an impeachment, from the practice in a writ of error, merely becaufe they are both *judicial*; for not only in thofe parts in which they are fuppofed to correfpond, but in every other circumstance, they are so totally dissimilar, that no two things in nature are so unlike. And you might with the same propriety pronounce upon the elegance and symmetry of a fine lady, from the form and proportions of a whale, because naturalists have placed them together in the same class of *Mammalia*.

This practice, with respect to appeals and writs of error, may be very useful and convenient; but it ought to have been introduced by an act of the Legislature, and not by the arbitrary *fiat* of the Lords themselves. It would be highly consistent with the dignity of the House of Commons, and conducive to the general interests of the kingdom, that they should examine witnesses upon oath; but it is to be hoped, that no oath will ever be administered there without the sanction of an Act of Parliament. That single instance might be wholesome and salutary; but, if they could do one lawless act for our benefit, they

they might do ten thousand for our destruction.

No one, I think, can doubt that the Court of the Lord High Steward begins and ends with the High Steward's commission, and therefore, if the commission should be dissolved before the conclusion of the trial, that it would be completely terminated; and I should even think that the indictment would be so annulled, that, if the trial of the Peer could be re-commenced, a fresh indictment must be found by a Grand Jury. This is a case which might easily happen, either by the death of the High Steward, or by the death of the King; for the continuation of this commission is not provided for by any Act of Parliament. And if the High Steward had proceeded with the trial till the Lords triers had pronounced a verdict of *guilty*, and then the commission had become vacated by death, if *autrefoits convict* is a good plea in bar, I should conclude that the convicted Peer could not afterwards receive judgment, nor consequently execution;

cution; and it would be precisely the case already mentioned before a Commissioner of Gaol-delivery. And what difference can be pointed out between a conviction before the High Court of Parliament, if their commission should cease before judgment is pronounced, and this case, I confess, I am unable to form a conjecture.

Mr. Justice Foster* has clearly shown, that in time of full Parliament the commission of a High Steward does not constitute any essential ingredient of the the jurisdiction of the Court, and that the Steward is appointed merely to add dignity and solemnity to the occasion.

But still it must be presumed, that his commission will be consistent with the writ or commission of the Peers; and therefore what is clear in the one, may fairly be admitted to explain what is doubtful in the other. Now the commission of the High Steward, both in cases of impeachments and in-

* 141, &c.

indictments before the High Court of Parliament, is exprefsly confined to the prefent Parliament; and the indifputable intent and meaning is, that the party muft be *heard, examined, fentenced,* and *adjudged,* in one and the fame Parliament. The words of part of his commiffion are thefe: " We, " confidering that juftice is an excellent " virtue, and pleafing to the Moft High, " and being willing that the faid Eliza- " beth,* of and for the felony whereof " fhe is indicted as aforefaid, *before us in* " *our prefent Parliament,* according to the " law and cuftom of our kingdom of " Great-Britain, may be *heard, examined,* " *fentenced,* and *adjudged,* and that all other " things neceffary may be executed, &c. " we have ordained and conftituted you " Steward of Great-Britain, &c. to execute " *for this time* the faid office."

The fame words of *coram nobis in præ- fenti Parliamento audiatur, fententietur, &*

adju-

* Duchefs of Kingfton, State Trials, Vol. XI. p. 198.

adjudicetur, are used in every High Steward's commission when a Peer has been impeached in the High Court of Parliament.

The words " for this time," or *pro hac vice*, certainly import that the High Steward shall execute his office during the whole of the trial; but the words *in præsenti Parliamento adjudicetur* restrain it to the present Parliament: so, if the impeachment or trial could continue beyond the present Parliament, this dilemma would ensue—either the Steward does not execute his office *pro hac vice*, or the party is not *in præsenti Parliamento adjudicatus*; and therefore a repugnancy would arise in the commission, and one part of the King's will must necessarily be frustrated.*

These solemn and ancient records have been held, by all Judges, in all times, the strongest evidence of what the law is; and it

---

* The reader would observe, in the Duke of Suffolk's impeachment, that the Commons request, over and over again, that the proceedings, &c. may be in the *present Parliament*, and *this same Parliament*, &c.

it can hardly be supposed that a commission which has issued upon the most awful occasions, when every iöta has been weighed, a commission which has always been executed by men of the most profound learning and splendid talents in the State, a commission too transcendent in its powers ever to be entrusted to a subject, but when the justice of the nation calls for it, should be composed in such a manner that any event should render it incongruous and absurd; and therefore it is not too much to conclude that no such event can exist.

There is one argument more which has been adopted upon this occasion, which I think it necessary to take notice of before I conclude, which is, that when the Parliament* took away the King's power to protect his favourites by granting them a pardon in the first instance, it virtually took away the King's prerogative of putting an end to the trial by a dissolution; for it is said, the abolition of one is to no purpose, if the other remains.

* 12 & 13 W. c. 2.

But it is an invariable rule in the construction of acts of Parliament, that the rights and prerogatives of the King cannot be altered or abridged by any statute, but where the King and those rights are expresly and specifically named. All the prerogatives of the King are sacred trusts reposed in him by the people, to be exercised for their benefit; and that the two Houses of Parliament may never steal from the King those valuable deposits by an inference or a stratagem, the Constitution has wisely pronounced, that they shall never, in any degree, be affected, but when they are fully and clearly described.

And after the recent proceedings in the year 1785, and the deliberate and almost unanimous decision of Lord Salisbury's case, this statute cannot possibly be produced as evidence that, as this prerogative was not removed at the same time, no one could entertain an opinion that the King possessed it.

It has been argued with much vehemence, that it is so dangerous a prerogative, that it is impossible such a monster can exist; but many monsters have had existence in our government; and it is only from their extirpation, by the arm of the legislature, that we enjoy our present happiness and security.

It has been described with all the force and energy of eloquence, what a lamentable and dreadful condition this country would be in, if the King possessed the power of preventing the impeachments of his Ministers by a dissolution; yet it is an unquestionable and indisputable truth, that if his Minister should be convicted of the most nefarious treasons against his Sovereign, and horrid machinations against the liberties of his country, the King can the next moment restore him to credit, and to his situation, as a public Minister of that country which he has irreparably injured, or attempted to injure. The King can ruin the country,

country, and save the greatest criminal from impeachment, by never calling a Parliament but once in three years; and then, only for the purpose of proroguing them for another three years: he can cancel all the criminal laws, by pardoning all crimes; he can debase the public money; he can put his negative upon the most salutary laws; he can appoint to public offices the worst and most ignorant of his subjects: but, notwithstanding the horrible consequences of these infinite powers, they not only exist, but they are peculiarly the favourites of the People of England. With perfect security they have reposed in the hands of the King, these sovereign prerogatives, these dearest of their own rights; convinced that a good King will exercise them for their happiness, and that a bad King dare not exert them for their destruction. The principle of self-preservation is a fundamental doctrine in the law of England; and that law which cautiously restrains me from brandishing my sword over the head of my Sovereign, or of the meanest of his

his subjects, permits me to wear it peaceably by my side, and, when the occasion requires it, to draw it for my defence.

However we may feel at the rude doctrine of cashiering Governors, or be charmed with brilliant disquisitions upon the abdication of Kings, I have always thought it a fact, too plain to be made clearer by argument, that the people of this country did dethrone James the Second, and did elect another King in his room; and that afterwards, to provide a successor to Queen Anne, they elected again one who had no right by inheritance, who had no right by previous election, and therefore who had no more right than any other man.

But they elected *him and his heirs*, I hope, I may add, *for ever*.—The People of England have experienced too much happiness from that choice, ever to admit the idea of another election, but as the last melancholy effort of desperation.

But the whole history of their ancestors will inform our Kings, that it can never conduce to their happiness or to their safety, to outrage the feelings of their people.

These I have always regarded as first and fundamental principles, which are only dangerous when they are treated with wantonness and levity.—The Majesty of the People (a grand expression, but brought into contempt by familiarity) ought never to be introduced but when the solemnity of the occasion demands it,—" Nec Deus in-
" terfit, nisi dignus vindice nodus inciderit." This awful attribute of the people ought to be mentioned with a reverence, little less than that with which we speak of the attributes of the Deity: but there is a doctrine which cannot be too familiar to our minds, and which we cannot too much cherish, *viz.* that, by the aid of the King, we can at any time cashier and elect our House of Commons.—It is this change which gives a perpetual motion to our Government, and preserves it incorruptible and immortal. If the Commons

were

were impiously to attempt to repeal Magna Charta, the *Habeas Corpus* Act, the Bill of Rights, and all that is dear to an Englishman, we should find it a much more arduous undertaking to compel a House of Commons, than to compel a King, to abdicate. But we are safe, while the King can listen to the voice of his people, and can, in an instant, annihilate those in whom they can no longer confide.

Charles the First never violated the Constitution more, by his opposition to Parliaments, than by his compliance, when he assented to an act that the two Houses of Parliament should dissolve themselves.

These are all the authorities and arguments which have occurred to the Author of this Examination in the course of his inquiry: and he can assure the Reader that he has suppressed nothing which he has thought material or relevant on either side; and however erroneous his own observations and constructions may be, he has stated nothing with an intent to mislead. The only prejudice which he feels upon the subject, is in favour of an opinion which he has collected with some degree of labour, and what arises from a natural anxiety to support that opinion, and to convince others of what he has convinced himself. And he cannot but indulge a hope, however delusive, that when this subject is better understood, the opinions of lawyers will be treated with more attention and respect, or rather, he should say, with less scorn and contempt: but he can affirm, of himself, that he is one who is solicitously desirous of being always thought a strenuous asserter of the dignity and privilege of Parliament, and a zealous advocate for the public justice of the Nation, but who, from some attention to the English Constitution, has taught himself that in this Country nothing can be *public Justice*, which is not administered by the hand of the *Law*.

APPENDIX.

APPENDIX.

Extracts from the Journals of the HOUSE *of* LORDS.

Die Martis, 11° *die Martii,* 1672.

ORDERED, by the Lords Spiritual and Temporal, in Parliament affembled, That it be referred to the Lords Committees for Privileges, to confider whether an appeal unto this Houfe (either by writ of error, or by petition) from the proceedings of any other court, being depending and not determined in one feffion of Parliament, continue in *ftatu quo* unto the next feffion of Parliament, without renewing the writ of error, or petition; and report their opinion unto the Houfe.

Die Sabbati, 29° *die Martii,* 1673.

Upon report made by the Lord Widdrington, from the Lords Committees for Privileges, &c. ' That, in
' purfuance of the matter referred to their Lordfhips
' by order of the 11th inftant (videlicet), whether an
' appeal unto this Houfe (either by writ of error or
' petition), or any other bufinefs wherein their Lordfhips

' ships act as in a court of judicature, and not in
' their legiflative capacity, being depending, and not
' determined in one feffion of Parliament, continue in
' *ſtatu quo*, unto the next feffion of Parliament, with-
' out renewing the writ of error or petition, or be-
' ginning all anew, their Lordſhips confidered feveral
' proceedings, both ancient and modern (which were
' produced to their Lordſhips at the Committee), *vi-
' delicet:*

' 1. In general: Crompton, Parliament 20. A ge-
' neral rule for writs of error depending, to be con-
' tinued to the next Parliament, and the writ of *ſcire
' facias* to be made then returnable.

' 2. In particular: 18 E. I. *Placita Parliamentaria*,
' p. 44 and 49, the cafe of William de Valentia and
' Ifabell Marefchall. William de Valentia had been
' impleaded, and put to anfwer, the Parliament before,
' which was prefently after Chriſtmas, at the fuit of
' Ifabell le Marefchall, for exercifing the office of a
' Sheriff in the Hundred of Hoftereflegh, he pleaded,
' he did it in the right of his wife, and that he ought
' not to be put to anfwer without her: whereupon
' he had time given for him and his wife to appear as
' this day, at this Parliament, beginning three weeks
' after Eafter; and Ifabell le Marefchall had the fame
' time given to profecute.

' The fame year, p. 43, Hugh de Louther's cafe;
' there being a queftion concerning lands held *in
' capite*, that had been formerly belonging to one
' Henry

'Henry de Edelyngthorp, then in the poffeffion of
'Henry de Louther as his heir; of which Thomas
' de Normanvill, the efcheator, was to give an account
' this Parliament, for recovering of the King's right
' upon that defcent; and one Adom coming and lay-
' ing claim to thofe lands, faying that he was right
' heir, the efcheator is ordered to make inquifition
' into it by a Jury, *ita quod ad proximum Parliamentum*
' *poft feftum S'ti Michaelis diftincte et aperte inde re-*
' *spondeat.*

' 21° E. I. p. 160. Magdulphus Earl of Fife had
' made his complaint, that John King of Scotland
' had unjuftly taken from him certain lands in the
' county of Fife. A writ of *fcire facias* was thereupon
' directed to the Sheriff of Northumberland, to warn
' the King of Scotland to appear before the King in
' Parliament fuch a day. The King of Scotland ap-
' peared, and made fome defence, which did not
' satisfy; fo they were pronouncing judgment againft
' him: but, before it was pronounced, he defired
' refpite till the next Parliament after Eafter, to advife
' with his Council in Scotland; and that then he
' would come (as he faid) *et feray ce que faire devray*,
' do what in duty he was to do. Upon which, day
' is given him till the next Parliament, which was to
' be after Eafter, *in omnibus eodem ftatu quo nunc.*

' 30 E. I. p. 234, the cafe of William de Breoufe
' and Walter de Pederton, conftable of Kermerdyn,
' touching the manor of Gower, for which William
' was fummoned in, to do fuit and fervice at the caftle

' of Kermerdyn ; of which he had complained, and
' day had been given to all parties to appear next Par-
' liament: and then it was not determined, but re-
' ferred to a further hearing at the following Parlia-
' ment, which was to be held at Lyncolne, in *Octabis*
' *Hillarii*; and from thence, after some debatings and
' arguings, put off again to this Parliament, in the
' 30th of the King, in *Octabis S'ti Johannis Baptistæ*,
' where the business was more fully heard, and course
' taken in it.

' The same year, p. 605, some merchants petition
' in Parliament for some debts owing to them, for
' which they have no other shewings but the court-
' rolls, which are in the keeping of the stewards and
' marshals, officers to the King, before whom those
' recognizances were taken, who refuse to shew them
' without special warrant; whereupon they are or-
' dered to bring all their court-rolls to the next Par-
' liament.

' 15 E. III. N. 8, 43, 49. The Archbishop of Can-
' terbury being arraigned in Parliament (according to
' his own desire) before his peers; the Bishops of Dur-
' ham and Sarum, and the Earls of Northumberland,
' Arundell, Warwick and Salisbury, were appointed
' to hear his answer, the same to be debated the next
' Parliament; and all things touching his arraign-
' ment to remain with Sir William of Keldesby,
' keeper of the privy seal.

' 51 E. III.

' 51 E. III. N. 96. Hugh Scaffolk, of Yarmouth,
' had been accufed, the Parliament before, of divers
' extortions; whereupon commiffion had been granted
' to the Earl of Suffolk and Sir John Cavendifh, chief
' juftice, to examine the bufinefs; and Sir John Ca-
' vendifh gave account in open Parliament, that by
' eighteen inquefts he had been found guiltlefs.

' 1 R. II. N. 28. The Earl of Salifbury, William
' de Mountacute, brings his writ of error upon a
' judgment in the King's Bench, by which Roger
' de Mortimer Earl of March, father to Edmond, had
' recovered from him fome lands in Wales. The
' record is brought into the Houfe by the Chief Juf-
' tice, there to remain; and a *fcire facias* awarded, to
' warn Edmond Earl of March to appear the next
' Parliament. The next Parliament, 2 R. II. N. 21,
' 22, 23, 24, the Earl of March appears; faith, the
' writ was not duly ferved, for that there was an
' error in the Sheriff's return; Edmond Mortimer,
' his grandfather, being there faid to be an Earl,
' which he never was. The Earl of Salifbury, on the
' other fide, affirmed it to be a good return. So, there
' being difficulty in the matter, and the Parliament
' drawing towards an end, day was given to both par-
' ties till next Parliament, with all advantages; and
' the matter to ftand as now it doth.

' 7 R. II. N. 20. The Prior and Convent of Mon-
' tague complain of a judgement given in the King's
' Bench, in behalf of Sir Richard Seymor, in which
' due form had not been obferved, and obtains to have
' them

' them amended: then prays the whole judgment to
' be reversed, for certain errors; and a *scire facias*, for
' Sir Richard to appear the next Parliament. All
' which was ordered; and the old process and record
' to be at the same next Parliament.

' 13 R. II. N. 15. Sir Thomas Metham brings a
' writ of error upon a judgment in the King's Bench,
' by which he was to pay five hundred marks to John
' Aske; and prays for a *scire facias*, returnable the
' next Parliament, for Aske then to appear. Which
' was granted.

' 15 R. II. N. 22. John Sheppy brings his writ of
' error for a judgment in the King's Bench, given in
' the behalf of the Prior of Huntington: ordered a
' *scire facias*, to warn the Prior to appear next Parlia-
' ment, to abide the order therein to be taken; and
' the whole record and process to be then there.

' N. 24. Edmond Boffett prays a *scire facias*, for a
' judgment given in the King's Bench, for several
' lands in the county of Sommersett, between the King
' demandant, and the said Edmond deforcient. Upon
' this petition, the *scire facias* is granted; and it is
' likewise ordered, that the matter shall continue in
' the same state until the next Parliament.

' 5 H. IV. N. 40. Roger Deyncourt complains of
' an erroneous judgment given against him in the
' King's Bench, for Ralph de Alderley; assigns the
' errors; then a *scire facias* is granted, for Alderley to
                                                    ' appear

' appear next Parliament. The next Parliament,
' 6 H. IV. N. 31. this *scire facias* is returned *tarde*
' *venit*; so a new one is granted, returnable the Par-
' liament after that, and the process to be continued.

' 1 H. V. N. 19. Gunwardby complains of a judg-
' ment in the King's Bench, in behalf of John Wind-
' sor, for several lands in Cambridgeshire; assigns the
' errors; hath a *scire facias* granted, to warn Windsor
' to appear at the next Parliament, to hear the record
' and process.

' 3 H. V. N. 19. Cathermaine prays a *scire facias*
' against William Hore and John Hore, executors of
' Thomas Hore, for an erroneous judgment given in
' the King's Bench, on the behalf of Thomas, upon
' an action of trespass: it is granted, returnable the
' next Parliament.

' 21 Jac. 28º *Maii*. The Lord Chief Justice brings
' into the House the record of judgment given here
' in the King's Bench, *in placito transgressionis et ejectio-*
' *nis firmæ*, between William Macdonnagh plaintiff,
' and John Farrar defendant, for lands in Ireland.
' Macdonnagh makes Thomas Stafford his attorney,
' by a letter there produced, and proved by two wit-
' nesses. Stafford assigns the errors; whereupon a
' writ is ordered, to go to the Chief Justice of Ireland,
' requiring him to issue out a writ of *scire facias* to
' the Sheriff of Wexford, to warn Farrar to appear
' before their Lordships at the next session of Parlia-
'   ' ment,

'ment, to hear the record and procefs of error in the
'judgment given in the King's Bench in that caufe.

'The fame day, the Earl of Bridgwater reports from
'the Committee for Petitions, the opinion of that
'Committee upon divers petitions, of which his Lord-
'ſhip did then give an account unto the Houfe; and
'it was, That they ſhould be retained in *ſtatu quo*
'until the next feſſion of Parliament, which was or-
'dered accordingly.

'Firſt Parliament of King Charles the Second,
'28 December, feveral petitions of Awbrey de Vere,
'Earl of Oxon, Charles Earl of Derby, and Thomas
'Lord Windfor, were read, concerning the office of
'the Great Chamberlain of England; and the Lords
'ordered, That the confideration of the faid petitions
'ſhould be adjourned to the fourth day of the ſitting
'of the next Parliament.

'The cafe of Dame Aliſimon Reade, the 4th of
'April, 1671, wife of Sir John Reade, praying to be
'relieved againſt the hard ufage of her huſband: it
'was ordered, that counfel on both parts ſhould be
'heard, on Thurfday the 6th of the fame April, on
'which day the Lords ordered, That the further de-
'bate of that bufinefs ſhould be adjourned to the firſt
'Tuefday of the next ſitting of the Parliament, after
'the recefs then at hand.

'The cafe of the Lord Delawarr, and the Lord
'Berkeley of Berkeley, concerning precedency, the

'14th

' 14th of April, 1671. It was ordered, that they
' should be heard on the second Monday of the next
' meeting of the Parliament after the recess."

Upon the consideration of these precedents, and of several others mentioned at the Committee, their Lordships came to a resolution, and accordingly declared it their opinion, That businesses depending in one Parliament, or session of Parliament, have been continued to the next session of the same Parliament, and the proceedings thereupon have remained in the same state in which they were left when last in agitation.

The House, taking the said report into their consideration, do approve thereof, and order it accordingly.

Die Martis, 11° *die Martii*, 1678.

It being moved, ' That this House would declare
' whether Petitions of Appeal, which were presented
' to this House in the last Parliament, be still in force
' to be proceeded on :'

It is ordered, by the Lords Spiritual and Temporal, in Parliament assembled, That it be and is hereby referred to the Lords Committees for Privileges, to consider thereof, and report their opinion thereupon, unto this House; and that the said Lords Committees do meet on Thursday next, at three of the clock in the afternoon, for that purpose.

Die Lunæ, 17° *die Martii,* 1678:

Ordered, by the Lords Spiritual and Temporal, in Parliament assembled, That it be, and is hereby, referred to the Lords Committees for Privileges to consider, Whether petitions of appeal, which were presented to this House in the last Parliament, be still in force to be proceeded on; as also to consider of the state of the impeachments brought up from the House of Commons last Parliament, and all incidents relating thereunto; and make report thereof unto the House.

Die Mercurii, 19° *die Martii,* 1678.

The House this day taking into consideration the report made from the Lords Committees for Privileges, That, in pursuance of the order of the 17th instant, to them directed, for considering whether petitions of appeal, which were presented to this House in the last Parliament, be still in force to be proceeded on, and for considering of the state of the impeachments brought up from the House of Commons the last Parliament, and all the incidents relating thereunto; upon which the Lords Committees were of opinion, That, in all cases of appeals and writs of error, they continue, and are to be proceeded on, in *statu quo,* as they stood at the dissolution of the last Parliament, without beginning *de novo;* and that the dissolution of the last Parliament doth not alter the state of the impeachments brought up by the Commons in that Parliament.

After

After some time spent in consideration thereof,

It is resolved, by the Lords Spiritual and Temporal, in Parliament assembled, That this House agrees with the Lords Committees in the said report.

Die Veneris, 22° *die Maii,* 1685.

Upon consideration of the cases of the Earl of Powis, Lord Arundell of Warder, the Lord Belasis, and the Earl of Danby, contained in their petitions.

After some debate,

This question was proposed, Whether the order of the 19th of March, $167\frac{8}{9}$, shall be reversed and annulled, as to impeachments?

The question being put, ' Whether this question
' should be now put?
It was resolved in the affirmative.

Then the question was put, ' Whether the order of
' the 19th of March, $167\frac{8}{9}$, shall be reversed and an-
' nulled, as to impeachments?'
It was resolved in the affirmative.

Dissentiente, John Earl of Radnor.

The Earl of Anglesey, before the putting of the above-said question, desired leave of the House to enter his dissent, if the question were carried in the affirmative; which was granted.

Several other Lords defired leave to enter their diffents.

' According to the right of peers to enter their
' diffent and proteftation againft any vote propounded
' and refolved upon any queftion in Parliament, we
' do enter our diffent and proteftation to the aforefaid
' vote or refolution; for thefe reafons, among many
' others:

' 1. Becaufe it doth, as we conceive, extra-judicially,
' and without a particular caufe before us, endeavour
' an alteration in a judicial rule and order of the Houfe,
' in the higheft point of their power and judicature.

' 2. Becaufe it fhakes and lays afide an order made
' and renewed upon long confideration, debate, report
' of committees, precedents, and former refolutions,
' without permitting the fame to be read, though
' called for by many of the Peers, and againft weighty
' reafons, as we conceive, appearing for the fame, and
' contrary to the practice of former times.

' 3. Becaufe it is inherent in every court of judica-
' ture, to affert and preferve the former rules of pro-
' ceedings before them, which therefore muft be fteady
' and certain, efpecially in this High Court; that the
' fubject and all perfons concerned may know how to
' apply themfelves for juftice. The very Chancery,
' King's Bench, &c. have their fettled rules and ftand-
' ing orders, from which there is no variation.

Anglefey
Clare
Stamford.

Die Sabbati, 5° *die Aprilis,* 1690.

Ordered, That on Wednesday next this House will take into consideration, 'Whether impeachments continue from Parliament to Parliament?'

Die Lunæ, 6° *die Octobris,* 1690.

Lords Committees appointed by the House to inspect and consider precedents, whether impeachments continue in *statu quo* from Parliament to Parliament; whose Lordships having considered thereof, are to report their opinions to this House.

Die Jovis, 30° *die Octobris,* 1690.

The Earl of Mulgrave reported from the Lords Committees appointed to inspect and consider precedents, whether impeachments continue in *statu quo* from Parliament to Parliament, several precedents concerning impeachments, brought to the Committee by Mr. Petyt from the Tower, as followeth:

Edw. III. 'Num. 1. Roger de Mortimer ⎫
A° 4.   'Num. 2. Symon de Berryford   All con-
          'Num. 3. John Matravers   demned
          'Num. 4. Bogo de Bayons,   ⎬ the same
                 Jn° Deverall   Parlia-
          'Num. 5. Tho. Gurny,   ment.
                 Will. Ogle   ⎭

        'Num. 16. Berkly, accused by the King,
          'found not guilty by twelve Knights;
          'yet, because the King was murdered
                                        'by

        'by persons under his command, was kept under bail till the next Parliament, which was A° 5; then he was discharged from his bail; and, A° 11, he is adjudged innocent; wherein also there is some mention made of proceedings about him A° 9, of which proceedings there is no record.

A° 15.   'Num. 8. 43. Archbishop of Cant. desires to be examined in Parliament; who is taken notice of again A° 17. Num. 22, where it is called an arraignment; but it is not plain that it was an impeachment, either from the King or the Commons.

A° 42.   'Num. 20. Jn° de la Lee, Steward of the Household.

A° 50.   'Num. 17. Rich. Lyons, merchant of London, impeached by the Commons, judged to prison till he paid a fine to the King.

        'On further enquiry, it was found, that he was awarded to prison at the will of the King, and put to fine and ransom according to the horribility of his offence, and to lose his franchise of the city of London.

A° 51.   'Memb. 27. Rot. Par. Afterwards he was pardoned in part by the Jubilee Pardon;

'don; but pardoned fully by a particu-
'lar pardon, for the procuring of which,
'Alice Pierce is accused in the first year
'of Rich. the Second.

A° 50.   'Num. 21. Lord Latimer, impeached by
'the Commons, had then judgment
'given on him; but not expressed what.
'Num. 31. 33. 34. William Ellis, Jn°
'Peachy, Lord Nevill, impeached by
'the Commons.
'Numb. 47. Adam de Bury impeached.

A° 51.   'Num. 91. The Commons desired he might
'be pardoned; and he had a particular
'pardon under the Great Seal.
'John Lester's was the same case.
'Num. 87. 89. 90. 92. Alice Pierce, Jn°
'de Lester, Walter Spurrier, were all
'condemned.

A° 50.   'Num. 95. 96. Hugh Farstaffs was ac-
'cused and acquitted, in A° 51 : Rich.
'IId Par. desired he might be restored
'to his favour, without any effect.

A° 1.   'Nu. 38. William de Weston, Jn° Sier de
'Gomine, condemned.
'Nu. 41. Alice Pierce accused and ba-
'nished.

A° 4.   'Num. 17. Sir Ra. Ferrers, accused by the
'King, acquitted; but put under bail
'to

'to appear before the King any time
between that and the next Parliament.'

A° 7. 'Par. 1. Num. 15. 23. 24. Bishop of Norwich, Sir Wm. Ellemhan, Sir Tho. Tryvet, Sir Hen. de Ferrers, Sir William de Farringdon, Rob't Fits Ralph Esquire, arraigned by the Commons, and condemned.

'Pars 2d. Nu. 11. Mich. De la Pool accused of bribery by Jn° Cavendish, and acquitted.

A° 10. 'Nu. 6. Accused by the Commons, condemned to be fined and imprisoned at the will of the King.

'Pars 1ª, Lords Appellants accused several Lords and Commoners, whom the Commons it seems themselves had a mind to impeach; which therefore they represent to the Lords, that proceedings might be stayed, who notwithstanding proceeded still in their own way.

'The Commons then impeach Sir Rob't Belknap Lord Chief Justice, Sir Jn° Cary Chief Baron, and other Judges, who were condemned the same Parliament.

'Memb. 10. Sir Symon De Burly, Sir Jn° Beauchamp, Sir Jn° Salisbury, Sir James Barners, impeached by the Commons, and adjudged.

A° 21.

A⁰ 21. Placita ⎫ 'Rot. Par. Duke of Gloucester, Earls
Coronæ. ⎭ 'of Arundell and Warwicke, ap‑
' pealed by the Earl of Rutland, be‑
' fore the King at Nottingham, and
' the proceedings brought into Par‑
' liament.
' Nu. 15. 19. Thomas Arundell, Archbishop of Cant.,
' Sir Tho. De Mortimer, accused by
' the Commons.

Hen. VI. ' Nu. 14. De la Pool Duke of Suffolke
A° 28. ' desired to have his fame vindicated in
' open Parliament, then impeached by
' the Commons, but not committed by
' the Lords, because it was a general
' accusation. At last there came a special
' accusation, upon which he was com‑
' mitted by the Lords, and banished by
' the King; against which proceeding
' and banishment all the Lords, Spiritual
' and Temporal, protested.

' The Committee sent for the Clerk of the Rolls,
' in order to find more precedents; the records in the
' Tower reaching no further, the Clerk accordingly
' attended, but said there was nothing registered there
' besides Acts of Parliament.

' Then the Committee examined the Journals of
' the House, which reach from the 12th of Hen. VII.
' and all the precedents of impeachments since that
' time are in a list now in the Clerk's hands; among
' all

'all which, none are found to continue from one
'Parliament to another, except the Lords who were
'lately so long in the Tower.

'The proceedings against the Lord Stafford were
'as follows:

CHARLES the IId.

A° 1678, Dec. 5. 'Impeached by the Commons.
Dec. 28. 'Examined.

In the next Parl. { 'April 9. Heard his accusation read.
1679.   { 'April 26. Put his answer in.

In another Parl. { 'Nov. 12. His trial appointed.
1680.   { 'Dec. 7. Condemned.

'The Committee also, in obedience to the House,
'sent for the late proceedings in the King's Bench in
'cases of impeachments, which are ready to be laid
'before the House, as well as all the extracts out of
'the records produced by Mr. Petyt.

'Then Mr. Petyt's Clerk, who attended by order,
'being called in, read the precedents following:

'Rot. Par. 4 E. III. N. 16. Thomas de Berkeley's
'case.

'Rot. Par. 15 E. III. N. 8. The Archbishop of
'Cant. case.

'And Rot. Clauf. 15 E. III. P. 3. M. 25. Dorf.
'prohibitio pro Rege.'

After the consideration of which precedents, &c. &c.
(as in the two last pages of this Appendix.)

                                     Die

Die Mercurii, 22° *Maii,* 1717.

Ordered, That all the Lords be a Committee to search for and report precedents.

Ordered, That it be an instruction to the said Committee, in the first place, to search for and report such precedents as relate to the continuance of impeachments from session to session, or from Parliament to Parliament.

Die Sabbati, 25° *Maii,* 1717.

The Lord Trevor (according to order) reported from the Committee, appointed to search and report such precedents, as may the better enable this House to judge what may be proper to be done, on occasion of the petition of the Earl of Oxford, and the case of the said Earl, as it now stands before this House,
' That, pursuant to the instruction given them, in the
' first place, to search for and report such precedents
' as relate to the continuance of impeachments from
' session to session, or from Parliament to Parliament,
' they had searched several precedents; and find,

' That, on the 6th of December 1660, an impeach-
' ment against William Drake, citizen and merchant
' of London, was brought from the Commons, and
' read; charging him with printing a seditious pam-
' phlet: and he was ordered to be apprehended as a
' delinquent.

' 12th December 1660, he was brought to the bar;
' and confessed he wrote the book mentioned in the
' articles.

' 19th

' 19th December, the said impeachment considered,
' it was ordered and declared, That, if this Parlia-
' ment be dissolved before this House have time to give
' judgment, the Attorney General should proceed
' against him at Law, upon the said offence.

' 3d Jan'y 1666, articles of impeachment, of high
' crimes, &c. were delivered, at a conference, against
' the Lord Viscount Mordaunt.

' 10th Jan'y, he was ordered to put in his answer.

' 17th Jan'y, he accordingly presented it.

' 7th Feb'y, a conference and free conference were
' had, concerning this impeachment.

' 8th Feb'y 1666, the Parliament was prorogued ;
' and no further proceeding on that impeachment
' after the prorogation.

' 24th April 1668, articles of impeachment, for high
' crimes, &c. against Sir William Penn, were delivered
' by the Commons, at a conference.

' 27th April, he was ordered to answer.

' 29th April, he delivered his answer, at the bar;
' and a copy of it was sent to the Commons.

' After two adjournments, by His Majesty's desire;
' the Parliament was, on the first of March 1668, pro-
' rogued, by commission, to the 19th of October fol-
' lowing ;

'lowing; and no more proceedings were had con-
'cerning the said impeachment.

'5th Dec'r 1678, Lord Arundell of Wardour, Earl
'of Powys, Lord Bellasis, Lord Petre, and Lord Vis-
'count Stafford, were impeached of high treason, &c.

'23d Dec'r, Earl of Danby was impeached of high
'treason; and articles were brought up.

'27th Dec'r, he was ordered to answer.

'The Parliament was dissolved by proclamation,
'dated 24th of January 1678.

'6th March 1678, a new Parliament met.

'13th of the same month, the Parliament was pro-
'rogued to the 15th of that month.

'17th of March, the House, considering whether
'the last prorogation made a session, were of opinion,
'That it was a session in relation to the acts of judi-
'cature, but not as to the determining laws deter-
'minable upon the end of a session. And the same
'day it was referred to the Committee for Privileges
'to consider, Whether petitions of appeal, presented
'last Parliament, be still in force to be proceeded on;
'and also to consider of the state of the impeachments
'brought up from the Commons last Parliament, and
'all the incidents relating thereto.

'18th

' 18th March, report was made from the said Com-
' mittee for Privileges, That, upon perusal of the
' Journal of the 29th of March 1673, they were of
' opinion, That, in all cases of appeals and writs of
' error, they continue and were to be proceeded on
' *in statu quo*, as they stood at the dissolution of the
' last Parliament, without beginning *de novo*; and also
' were of opinion, That the dissolution of the last
' Parliament did not alter the state of the impeach-
' ments brought up by the Commons in that Parlia-
' ment.

' 19th March, that report was considered; and,
' upon the question, was agreed to.

' 20th of March 1678, the Earl of Danby was or-
' dered to answer; and divers further proceedings
' were had upon the said impeachments, in that and
' subsequent Parliaments.

' 12th Nov'r 1680, the Commons, by message, ac-
' quaint the Lords with their resolution to proceed to
' the trial of the Lords in the Tower, and forthwith
' to begin with Viscount Stafford; and to desire a day
' for his trial.

' Whereupon his trial was appointed on the 30th
' instant.

' 30th of the same Nov'r, his Lordship's trial began
' in Westm'r Hall.

' 4th

'4th Dec'r following, the Lord High Steward gave
the House an account, That, after Viscount Stafford
had summed up his evidence, and the Managers had
replied, his Lordship propounded several points in
law, arising out of the matter of fact, to which he
desired to be heard by his counsel; one of which
points was,

> 'Whether proceedings ought to be continued from
> Parliament to Parliament upon impeachments?

'To which the House, upon consideration, refused to
hear his counsel.

'7th Dec'r, judgment upon him was pronounced,
as usual in cases of high treason.

'21st of the same month, Mr. Seymour was impeached of high crimes, &c.; and articles were
brought up, and read; and he was ordered to answer.

'23d of the same December, he put in his answer;
and the same was read, while he was at the bar;
and a copy of it to be sent to the Commons.

'3d Jan'y following, which was the next day the
House sat, he petitioned for a speedy trial. And a
message was sent to the Commons, to give them notice of it; their Lordships finding no issue joined by
replication. And counsel were assigned him.

'8th Jan'y, his trial was ordered to be on the 15th
of the same January; and a message was sent to the
'Commons,

' Commons, to acquaint them with it, that they might
' reply if they thought fit. No further proceeding
' was had on that impeachment.

' 7th of the same January, Sir William Scroggs
' was impeached of high treason; and articles of im-
' peachment were brought up. He was bailed; and
' ordered to answer the 14th of the same month.

' The said 7th of January, the Earl of Tyrone was
' impeached of high treason.

' 10th of Jan'y 1680, the Parliament was pro-
' rogued; and dissolved by proclamation the 18th of
' that month.

' 21st March 1680, a new Parliament met.

' 24th of the same March, Earl of Danby petitioned
' to be bailed: and the same day Sir William Scroggs'
' answer was read; as also his petition, desiring a
' short day for the Commons to reply; copies of
' which answer and petition were sent to the Com-
' mons.

' No further proceedings were had against Sir Wil-
' liam Scroggs.

' 26th March 1681, message from the Commons,
' That they, having formerly demanded judgment
' against the Earl of Danby, desire now a day may be
' appointed to give it.

                                              ' The

'The said message was ordered to be considered on
' Monday next.

' 28th of the same month, the Parliament was dis-
' solved.

' 19th May 1685, the House was acquainted, That
' the Lords committed to the Tower upon impeach-
' ment had entered into recognizances, in the King's
' Bench, to appear the first day of next Parliament;
' which was that day. Accordingly they were called
' to the bar, and their appearances recorded; and
' they petitioned for relief.

' 22d May 1685, upon consideration of the cases of
' the Earl of Powys, Lord Arundell, Lord Bellasis,
' and Earl of Danby, contained in their petitions, it
' was resolved, upon the question, That the order of
' the 19th of March 167$\frac{8}{9}$ should be annulled and re-
' versed as to impeachments.

' 25th May 1685, an order made, for the Attorney
' General to have recourse to the indictments against
' the Earl of Powys, Lord Arundell, and Lord Bel-
' lasis, in order to the entering a *noli prosequi* thereon,
' according to His Majesty's warrant; and it was fur-
' ther ordered, that their bail should be discharged.

' 1st June 1685, upon motion on behalf of several
' Peers, who were bail for the appearance of the Earl
' of Powys, Earl of Danby, Lord Arundell, Lord
' Bellasis, and Earl of Tyrone in the Kingdom of
Ireland,

'Ireland, the first day of this Parliament, whose re-
'cognizances were entered into in the King's Bench;
'it was ordered, That the said Lords, as also all per-
'sons, Peers or others, that were bailed for their ap-
'pearance, should be discharged.

'26th October 1698, the Earl of Salisbury and Earl
'of Peterborow were impeached of high treason, in
'departing from their allegiance, and being recon-
'ciled to the Church of Rome, by message from the
'Commons. And the Earl of Peterborow being, by
'the Black Rod, brought to the bar, was ordered to
'be committed to the Tower; and the Earl of Salis-
'bury to be brought to the bar, by the Chief Gover-
'nor of the Tower, on Monday.

'28th October, the Earl of Salisbury accordingly
'was brought to the bar; and the said Governor of
'the Tower was ordered to take him into his custody.

'27th Jan'y following, the Parliament was pro-
'rogued; and dissolved by proclamation the 6th of
'February following.

'A new Parliament met, 20th of March 1689.

'5th April 1690, an order was made, to take into
'consideration, whether impeachments continue from
'Parliament to Parliament, on the Wednesday fol-
'lowing.

'8th and 10th of the same month, consideration of
'that matter was adjourned.

'7th

' 7th July 1690, the Parliament was prorogued.

' 2d October 1690, the Earl of Peterborow peti-
' tioned to be discharged, having been kept prisoner in
' the Tower for almost two years, notwithstanding a
' dissolution and several prorogations had intervened,
' as also an act of free and general pardon : where-
' upon the Judges were ordered to attend, to give their
' opinions, whether he be pardoned by that act. The
' Judges were also ordered to give their opinions, on
' the same matter, upon the Earl of Salisbury's petition,
' praying likewise to be discharged.

' 6th of the same month, the Judges, according to
' order, delivered their opinions, as follow; viz. That,
' if the said Earls crimes and offences were committed
' before the 13th of February 1688, and not in Ire-
' land, nor beyond the seas, they were pardoned by
' the said act; and it was resolved, that the said Earls
' should be admitted to bail. And a Committee was
' appointed to inspect and consider precedents, whe-
' ther impeachments continue *in statu quo* from Parlia-
' ment to Parliament.

' 7th October, the said Earls were both bailed at
' the bar.

' 30th of the same October, report was made from
' the Committee, appointed the 6th of the same Octo-
' ber, of several precedents brought to their Lordships
' by Mr. Petyt from the Tower; and also that they

' had

' had examined the Journals of this House, which
' reach from the 12th of Henry the VIIth; and all
' the precedents of impeachments since that time were
' in a list now in the Clerk's hands; among all which,
' none are found to continue from one Parliament to
' another, except the Lords who were lately so long
' in the Tower.

' After consideration of which report, and reading
' the orders made the 19th of March 167$\frac{8}{9}$, and the
' 22d of May 1685, concerning impeachments; and
' long debate thereupon; it was resolved, That the
' Earl of Salisbury and Earl of Peterborow should be
' discharged from their bail; and accordingly they and
' their sureties were ordered to be discharged from
' their said recognizances.

' A list has been produced before the Committee,
' which to them seems to be the list referred to in the
' said report; which is ready to be produced, if the
' House shall think the same necessary.

' 12th Nov'r 1650, upon motion, ' That a day be
' appointed, for the explanation of the votes of the
' 30th of October last;' it was ordered to take the
' same into consideration on the 18th of the same No-
' vember, and all the Lords to be summoned; on
' which day the House sat: but it doth not appear by
' the Journal that any thing was done in pursuance of
' that order.

' 27th April 1695, the Duke of Leeds was im-
' peached of high crimes and misdemeanors; and arti-
' cles

' cles were on the 29th of the same month exhibited
' against him. He put in his answer the next day;
' and a copy of it was sent to the Commons.

' 1st May following, a message was sent to the
' Commons, to put them in mind of the said impeach-
' ment; the Lords conceiving the session could not
' continue much longer.

' 3d of the same May, the Parliament was pro-
' rogued; and dissolved by proclamation, dated the
' 11th of October 1695.

' 24th of June 1701, the House of Commons hav-
' ing impeached the Duke of Leeds on the 27th of
' April 1695; and on the 29th of the same month
' exhibited articles against him, to which he answered;
' but the Commons not prosecuting, the said im-
' peachment and articles were ordered to be dismissed.

' 17th May 1698, Peter Longueville was, amongst
' others, impeached of high crimes, &c.; and articles
' were brought up.

' 27th of the same May, he put in his answer, and
' pleaded Not Guilty.

' 28th June, the trial of Goudet and others, upon
' the impeachments against them, was appointed on
' the 4th of July next.

' The same day, the said Goudet, Barrau, Seignoret,
' Baudowin, Santiny, Diharce, and Pearse, relin-
' quished

' quifhed their pleas, and pleaded Guilty; and the
' Black Rod ordered to take them into cuftody.

' 30th June, Dumaiftre put in his anfwer, and
' pleaded Guilty; and the Black Rod ordered to take
' him into cuftody.

' 4th July 1698, judgment was pronounced againft
' the eight perfons above mentioned; and no further
' proceedings concerning Longueville.

' The next day the Parliament was prorogued; and
' diffolved by proclamation, dated the 7th of July
' 1698.

' The Committee have alfo inquired of precedents
' of indictments againft Peers, which have been re-
' moved into the Houfe of Lords by *Certiorari*, and
' the proceedings thereupon; and find, that, on the
' 19th of March 1677, the proceedings againft the
' Earl of Pembroke, upon an indictment, for the death
' of Nathaniel Cony, had before the commiffioners of
' Oyer and Terminer at Hicks' Hall, upon which his
' Lordfhip was found guilty of felony and murder,
' was brought into this Houfe, in order to his trial.

' 4th April 1678, the faid Earl was tried, and found
' guilty of manflaughter.

' 15th July following the Parliament was prorogued.

' 11th Nov'r 1685, the Lord Mayor and the reft
' of the Juftices of Oyer and Terminer and General
' Gaol

'Gaol Delivery for London and Middlesex were or-
'dered to return, by virtue of His Majesty's writ of
'*Certiorari*, the indictment of high treason, found
'before them, against the Earl of Stamford, then
'prisoner in the Tower.

'14th Nov'r, the indictment was delivered.

'16th Nov'r, the said Earl was ordered to be
'brought to the bar.

'17th Nov'r, his Lordship was brought according-
'ly, examined, and his trial appointed on the 1st of
'December following; and an address to His Ma-
'jesty, That a place be prepared in Westm'r Hall for
'his trial.

'18th Nov'r, the King's answer was reported,
'That He had given order accordingly.

'20th Nov'r 1685, the Parliament was prorogued;
'and, after several prorogations, was dissolved the
'2d of July 1687.

'And there doth not appear any further proceeding
'on the said indictment.

'4th Jan'y 1692, the Coroner's Inquest was brought
'in, concerning the death and murder of William
'Mountfort, wherein the Lord Mohun was found
'to be aiding and assisting.

'4th Feb'y following, his Lordship was tried; and
'found Not Guilty, and discharged.

'14th

' 14th March following, the Parliament was pro-
' rogued.

' 13th Dec'r 1697, a writ of *Certiorari* was ordered,
' for removing the indictment found against the Lord
' Mohun, concerning the death of William Hill.

' 10th Jan'y 1697, refolved to proceed to his trial.

' 4th July 1698, the Clerk of the Crown read the
' indictment to his Lordship; and he pleaded His
' Majefty's pardon: which was allowed by the Houfe;
' and he was difcharged.

' 13th March 1698, an indictment againft the Earl
' of Warwick, for the murder of Coote, was brought
' by *Certiorari*.

' 25th March 1699, Lord Mohun allowed a copy
' of his indictment.

' 28th March, the Earl of Warwick was tried, and
' found guilty of manflaughter.

' 29th of the fame month, the Lord Mohun was
' tried, and found Not Guilty.

' 4th May 1699, the Parliament was prorogued.'

Which report being read by the Clerk:

It was propofed, ' To refolve, That the impeach-
' ment of the Commons againft the Earl of Oxford
' is determined by the intervening prorogation.'

' And,

And, after debate thereupon,

The question was put, 'That it is the opinion
'of this House, that the impeachment exhi-
'bited by the Commons of Great Britain,
'against Robert Earl of Oxford and Earl Mor-
'timer, for high treason and other high crimes
'and misdemeanors, is determined by the in-
'tervening prorogation.'

It was resolved in the negative.

Dissentient,

' 1. Because there seems to be no difference in law
' between a prorogation and a dissolution of a Parlia-
' ment, which, in constant practice, have had the
' same effect, as to determination both of judicial and
' legislative proceedings; and consequently this vote
' may tend to weaken the resolution of this House,
' May the 22d, 1685, which was founded upon the
' law and practice of Parliament in all ages, without
' one precedent to the contrary; except in the cases
' which happened after the order made the 19th of
' March 1678, which was reversed and annulled in
' 1685; and in pursuance hereof the Earl of Salisbury
' was discharged in 1690.

' 2. Because this can never be extended to any but
' Peers; for, by the statute 4° Ed. III[ii], no Commoner
' can be impeached for any capital crime: and it is
' hard to conceive why the Peers should be distin-
' guished, and deprived of the benefit of all the laws
' of liberty to which the meanest Commoner in Britain

' is entitled; and this seems the more extraordinary,
' because it is done unasked by the Commons, who,
' as it is conceived, never can ask it with any colour
' of law, precedent, reason, or justice.

'NOTTINGHAM.
'ABINGDON.
'FR. ROFFEN.
'NORTH & GREY.
'BRUCE.
'DARTMOUTH.
'BATHURST.
'GUILFORD.
'MANSEL. HAY.
'FOLEY.'

Die Martis, 24° *Junii,* 1701.

Then the House, taking into consideration that there were several Lords charged and impeached by the Commons, and no prosecution against them, ordered as followeth (videlicet).

The House of Commons not having prosecuted their charge which they brought up against John Lord Haversham, for words spoken by him at a free conference the thirteenth instant;

It is this day ordered, by the Lords Spiritual and Temporal in Parliament assembled, That the said charge

charge against John Lord Haversham shall be, and is hereby, dismissed.

The Earl of Portland being impeached, by the House of Commons, of high crimes and misdemeanors, the first day of April last:

It is ordered by the Lords Spiritual and Temporal in Parliament assembled, That the impeachment against William Earl of Portland shall be, and is hereby, dismissed, there being no articles exhibited against him.

The House of Commons having impeached Charles Lord Hallifax, of high crimes and misdemeanors, on the fifteenth day of April last, and on the fourteenth day of this instant June exhibited articles against him; to which he having answered, and no further prosecution thereupon:

It is ordered by the Lords Spiritual and Temporal in Parliament assembled, That the said impeachment and the articles exhibited against him shall be, and they are hereby, dismissed.

The House of Commons having impeached Thomas Duke of Leeds of high crimes and misdemeanors on the seven and twentieth of April, one thousand six hundred ninety-five, and on the nine and twentieth of the said April exhibited articles against him; to which he answered: but the Commons not prosecuting,

It is ordered by the Lords Spiritual and Temporal in Parliament aſſembled, That the ſaid impeachment and the articles exhibited againſt him ſhall be, and they are hereby, diſmiſſed.

Rotul. Parl. XV. Edw. III.

Le Parlement tenuz a Weſtm' le Lundy en la Quinzeyne de Paſch', l'an du regne n're Seignur le Roi, c'eſt aſſaver d'Engleterre Quinziſme, et de France Second.

8. ET meiſme ceſti jour vient noſtre Seignur le Roi en la Chaumbre de Peynte, & illocques vient l'Erceveſque de Cantirburs, & les autres Prelatz, & Grantz, & Communes; & le dit Erceveſque ſe humilia a n're Seignur le Roi, enquerant ſa bone Seignurie & ſa bienvoilliance; et n're Seignur le Roi lui reſceut a ſa bone Seignurie: dont les Prelatz & autres Grantz lui mercierent tant come ils ſavoient ou purroient. Et puis pria l'Erceveſque au Roi, q'il pleuſt a ſa Seignurie, que deſicome il eſt diffamez notoirement par tut le Roialme & aillours, q'il puiſſe eſtre ateſnez en pleyn Parlement devant les Pieres, & illocques reſpoundre, iſſint, q'il ſoit overtement tenuz pur tiel come il eſt. Queu choſe le Roi ottreia. Mes il dit, q'il voleit que les buſoignes touchantes l'eſtat du Roialme & commune profit fuſſent primes mys en exploit, & puis il feroit exploiter les autres.

APPENDIX. xxxvii

43. ET fait remembrer, que le Samady, en la Veille de Pentecouft, feurent acordez & affentuz en dit Parlement les chofes fouzefcrites, c'eft affaver.

44. Primerement, que les Evefques de Durefme, & Sarum, les Countes de Norht', Arundell, Warr', & Sarum, oient les Refpons l'Ercevefque, des chofes qui lui font furmys par le Roi; iffint que fi fes dites Refpons foient covenables, adonques le Roi de fa bone grace lui tendra pur excufe. Et en cas q'il femble au Roi & a fon Confeil, que meifmes les Refpons ne font mye fuffifantz, adonques les ditz Refpons ferront debatuz en prefchein Parlement, & illocques ent juggement rendu.

49. ET fait a remembrer, que totes les chofes touchantes l'Arefnement l'Ercevefque de Cantirburs, demurent devers S. William de Hyldefby, Gardeyn du Prive Seal notre Seignur le Roi.

Rotul. Par. XVII. Edw. III.

Le Parlement le tenuz a Weftm'r, a la Quinzeyne de Pafk, l'an du Regne n're Seign' le Roi Edward tiercz apres le Conqueft, c'eft affaver d'Enleterre dys & feptifme, & de France quart,

22. FAIT a remembrer, que notre Seign' le Roi ad commandez, que totes les chofes touchantes l'arreynement . . . . . l'Ercevefque de Cantirbirs, lefqueux chofes demurerent devers Seign' William de
Kyldefby,

Kyldesby, au Parlement tenuz a Westm' a la quinzeyne de Paske lan quinzisme pur aver ent avisement tan que ne sont pas resonables ne veritables. Par quoi comande fu a Mestre Johan de Ufford, de porter meismes les choses en Parlement pur anienter illoeques.

Commons' Journals.

Die Sabbati, 12° *die Aprilis*, 1679.

Sir Francis Winnington reports from a conference.—

The Lord Privy Seal said, that in the transaction of this affair, there were two great points gained by this House of Commons.

The first was, that impeachments made by the Commons in one Parliament, continued from session to session, and from Parliament to Parliament, notwithstanding prorogations or dissolutions.

The other point was, that in cases of impeachments upon special matter shewn, if the modesty of the party impeached directs him not to withdraw, the Lords admit that of right they ought to order him to withdraw; and that afterwards he must be committed.

The Commons replied, that they hoped their Lordships did not think the Commons did take it, as if they had now gained any point: for that the points which their Lordships mentioned as gained, were nothing but what was agreeable to the ancient course and methods of Parliament.

My Lord of Danby's Cafe, Skinner's Reports; *p.* 56, 34 *Car.* II. R. B.

The *Earl of Danby* having been twice before in Court, upon his *Habeas Corpus*, came again this term, and made a very long harangue; but the Court would not bail him, his cafe being the fame with my Lord *Stafford*'s and the Earl of *Tyrone*'s, fcil. he was committed by the *Lords* Houfe, and there was an impeachment by the *Commons* pending in the Lords Houfe againft him; but it was taken clearly by the *Court*, that where the party is committed by an order of the *Lords* Houfe, as in Pritchard's cafe, remembered by *Raymond* Juftice, 17 Car. II. that upon a *prorogation* he may be bailed. And fo *Pemberton*, Chief Juftice, faid it was his cafe, he was committed by the Commons: he faid the *King* was willing to bail him, and fo were the Lords; but he was fain to lie, till the King prorogued the Parliament; and then he came out, and he faid, that if any one be detained after a *prorogation*, an *action of falfe imprifonment* lies; moreover, 'twas faid, that no man could come into that *Court* and demand to be bailed *de jure*, in cafe of *high treafon*; nay, that in murder fometimes they take bail, and fometimes refufe it.

My Lord Danby's Cafe, Skinner's Reports, *p*. 162, 35 *and* 36 *Car.* II. R. B.

Things chiefly infifted on by the *Counfel* and *Judges* in my Lord *Danby*'s cafe.—Wallop, That this was a cafe of great neceffity, and if there fhould be no

relief

relief here, there would be a failure of juſtice, which, rather than the law will ſuffer, it will allow things to be done contrary to the expreſs words of an Act of Parliament; and cited the 2 Inſt. 25.

That bailing would not affect the impeachment, but only modify the confinement; for they ſhould not deliver him out of cuſtody, but only lengthen his chain; for his bail, if they pleaſe, may keep him, and confine him: that all impriſonment is either in *cuſtodiam*, or in *pœnam*; where 'tis the former, this Court may give eaſe by bailment; but in ſo doing, they determine not *de re* but *de modo rei* or *de modo modi*: that this Court is the Supreme Court of ordinary Judicature, to which no ſubject can come but he finds relief, and that *Curia regis ne deficeret in juſtitia exhibenda*; the King being the fountain of juſtice, no one ſhall come to this fountain and die for thirſt. He cited the caſes where the Court hath bailed in caſe of extreme old-age, though the party was in execution; and ſo of a woman near her time of travail: Which caſes are in the 1ſt Inſt.

Pollexfen inſiſted that it was a caſe judicially in the Houſe of Lords; and then by diſſolution of Parliament the proceeding is determined, like caſes of writs of error out of the King's Bench. Holt cited the caſe of Okey and Baxter, who were attainted by Act of Parliament, and the records of Parliament removed by *certiorari* in Chancery, thence by *mittimus* into R. B. where the parties were oppoſed, wherefore they ſhould

not

not be executed, and were executed accordingly; and after, by the unanimous opinion of the Court, the Lord *Danby* was bailed.

For, *First*, Treason cannot be committed but against the King.

Secondly, That the Court has power to bail in all cases of treason. *Zachary Crofton*'s case, the opinion of the Judges, in the Lords House, 1678.

Thirdly, That when the Lords House is sitting, the power of this Court is suspended, as to persons and causes before them; but when the Lords House is dissolved, their original power reverts back to this Court.

Fourthly, This Court may bail, in cases where they cannot try the party bailed; as persons taken here for offences committed in Ireland, are bailed here, to appear in Ireland, though they cannot be tried here: so any *Lord of Parliament* committed for high treason by a Justice of Peace, or Secretary of State, may be bailed in R. B. though he cannot be tried there.

Fifthly, For a man committed of high treason to be bailed by law, and yet no Court in being that hath power to bail him, is an absurdity.

Sixthly, That in cases of writs of error depending in Parliament, upon a *long prorogation*, they cease to
be

be a *superfedeas*, but the party may have execution in R. B. and if it be so, but where the property is concerned, it ought much more to be so, where the liberty is concerned, which is so much dearer; that in one case or the other, the Parliament, when it meets, may go on; and, if they reverse the judgment, the party will be restored to all that he has lost, and so they may proceed to the trial of my Lord Danby, &c.

As to the power of the King's pardoning treason, though the person was impeached by the *Commons in England* in the Lords House, many records were cited by the Lord *Danby*; and *Pollexfen*, and *Jefferies*, *Chief Justice*, cited *Elsing* of *Parliaments*, and insisted that the *Habeas Corpus Act* shews the intent of the Parliament, and their sentiments in such cases.

Lord Salisbury's Case, Carthew, *p.* 131. 2 *Wil.* and *Mary*, B. R.

He was brought from the Tower by Habeas Corpus, and being at the bar, his case was thus:

He was by the convention which was afterwards turned into a Parliament, Anno 1 W. and M. impeached by the Commons for high treason, for being reconciled to the Church of Rome, contrary to the statute in that case made and provided, and upon this impeachment he was committed to the Tower by the House of Peers, and there continued till the Parliament was dissolved, and a new Parliament called, and

and now (after a long seffions) adjourned for two months.

The Counsel for the Earl moved, that he might be discharged upon the new Act of Oblivion, which passed in the last seffions of Parliament, wherein neither his crime nor his person were excepted, but clearly within the Act of Pardon. But *per curiam:* notice cannot be taken of this Act of Pardon, unless 'tis pleaded with the averments, because there are several exceptions in it, both as to crimes and persons; therefore it is necessary that the party who would have the benefit thereof, should aver himself by plea capable of such benefit; and not excepted therein, as 'tis ruled in Plowden, and other books; and here the Lord at the bar cannot plead this pardon, because there is nothing before the Court, upon which to ground such plea.

Then it was moved, that he might be bailed, and for that purpose the Lord Danby's case was cited, who was bailed, though committed by the Peers in Parliament, as in this case; and the Earl of Shaftesbury's case was likewise mentioned.

Sed per curiam: The Earl of Salisbury was not bailed, because there was a very short adjournment of the present Parliament, and that is the proper place for him to make application to be bailed.

That the chief reason for bailing the Lord Danby was, because the then Parliament were prorogued, and the time uncertain for their meeting again; and so no prospect of an opportunity to apply himself that way: besides, he was denied to be bailed, by several Judges of the Court of B. R. until the Chief Justice Jefferies came in.

And the Court cited the Lord Stafford's case, who was committed by the House of Peers; and notwithstanding that Parliament was dissolved, by which he was committed, yet he was continued a prisoner, and afterwards tried upon the same impeachment, convicted, and executed; which fully proves that commitments by the Peers in Parliament, are not made void by the prorogation or dissolution of the same Parliament.

Besides, the Lord Danby was bailed to appear at the next Sessions of Parliament, which was an affirmance of the commitment, and a plain proof of the opinion of the Court at that time, that the commitment was not avoided or discharged by the prorogation of the Parliament.

And for these reasons, the Lord Salisbury was remanded to the Tower.

Extract from Mr. Justice Foster's *Crown Law, p.* 157.

In the case of Lord Salisbury, who had been impeached by the Commons for high treason, the Lords, upon his petition, allowed him the benefit of the act of general pardon, passed in the second year of William

liam and Mary, so far as to discharge him from his imprisonment, upon a construction they put upon that act; *no High Steward ever having been appointed in that case.*

On the 2d of October, 1690, upon reading the Earl's petition, setting forth, that he had been a prisoner for a year and nine months in the Tower, notwithstanding the late act of free and general pardon, and praying to be discharged; the Lords ordered the Judges to attend on the Monday following, to give their opinions, Whether the said Earl be pardoned by the act. On the 6th, the Judges delivered their opinions, that if his offence was committed before the 13th of February 1688, and not in Ireland, or beyond the seas, he is pardoned. Whereupon it was ordered, that he be admitted to bail; and the next day he and his sureties entered into a recognizance of bail, himself in 10,000l. and two sureties in 5000l. each; and on the 30th, he and his sureties were, after a long debate, discharged from their recognizance.

It will not be material to inquire, whether the House did right in discharging the Earl without giving the Commons an opportunity of being heard; since, in fact, they claimed and exercised a right of judicature without an High Steward, *which is the only use I make of this case.*

MODERN

MODERN REPORTS, Vol. XII. p. 604, 13 W. III.
B. R.

Peters verſus *Benning.*

A writ of error *ad proximam ſeſſionem* in Parliament, and before that time the Parliament by proclamation was diſſolved, and day fixed for the meeting of a new one; and upon motion, the queſtion was, Whether this writ were a ſuperſedeas of execution, or even could be a warrant to ſend up the record to the new Parliament, there being no term intervening between the return of the writ and the time fixed for the Parliament's meeting. And, 1ſt, it was agreed on, that the Court can take no notice of any extrajudicial determination or order of the Lords. And, *per Holt*, If an impeachment be in one Parliament, and ſome proceedings thereon, and then the Parliament be diſſolved, and a new one called, there may be a continuance upon the impeachment; and he quoted the caſe of *James and Bertly*, *Paſch.* 5 *W. and M.* where a writ of error was teſted the fourth of May, returnable the nineteenth of November following, to which time the Parliament was prorogued, ſo that a whole term intervened; and he ſaid it was his opinion, they might ſue out execution, notwithſtanding that writ. And he remembered to have known it ruled in *Keeling* and *Hale*'s time, that a writ of error was no *ſuperſedeas*, after a prorogation, if a term intervened. *Vide* 3 *Keb.* 416. 1 *Vent.* 266. And the caſe in 2 *Cro.* 341. was ſaid to be in point, that a writ of error, and all the
proceed-

proceedings thereon, are determined by the diffolution of a Parliament. *Vide* Lane, 57. 1 H. VII. 19, 20. pl. 50. Br. Err. pl. 25. That plaintiff in error is not bailable in Parliament for two reafons; one, That if the judgment fhould be affirmed, they could not award execution on the recognizance; Secondly, If the Parliament fhould be diffolved before any thing done, all matter depending before the Parliament would be thereby determined. Likewife a tranfcript of the record, and not the very record itfelf, is before the Lords upon a writ of error; and in that it differs from a writ of error from Ireland, or from the C. B. into this Court, where, in the one cafe, the execution is to be awarded here; but in the other cafe, it is not fo, for the neceffity of the thing, becaufe the King's writ runs not into Ireland; the courfe is to fend a mandate to the Chief Juftice of Ireland to grant execution. *Vide Jo.* 66. That diffolution determines error actually depending, *Ray.* 5. That a prorogation and a whole term intervening, is a *fuperfedeas* of a writ of error in Parliament; and fo of a diffolution, though the errors had been affigned. If, before the tranfcript be left above, the Parliament was diffolved, the writ was no *fuperfedeas* of execution; but if it had been left above, the diffolution would be a *fuperfedeas* of it: but the writ of error would not be difcontinued, there being a day certain for the meeting of a new Parliament, by the very act of diffolution.

It may be a queftion, if a writ of error *ad proximum Parliamentum*, when a Parliament is to meet at a day certain, be a *fuperfedeas*, though a term does

not

not interpofe between the tefte of the writ and the time fixed for the meeting of the Parliament by the diffolution of the former Parliament; but the Chief Juftice faid, that as the prefent cafe was, the writ in queftion could not be an authority to carry up the record, neither could the Lords be legally poffeffed of it, by virtue of that writ. And he faid, in cafe of prorogation, the writ of error was returnable *ad præfens Parliamentum*; but in cafe of adjournment, it was *ad præfentem feffionem*. And after all, here the Court left them to do what they could by law.

Rot. Parl. 8 Hen. VI. n. 27.

ITEM priount les Communes, pur tant que lour fuft declarre en ceft prefent Parlement, par diverfes Seigneurs de mefme le Parlement, que lez petitions a baillers par les ditz Communes a tres noble & puiffant Prince le Duc de Gloucefter, Gardeyn d'Engleterre, en ceft prefent Parlement, ne ferroient mye engroffes avaunt ceo q'ils ferrount envoiez de par delà le Myer, a no're Soverayne Seignur le Roy, pur ent avoir foun affent Roiall & advys; que pleafe a dit tres haut & puiffant Prince le Duc de Glouc', Gardeyn d'Engleterre, de ordeiner par auctorite de ceft prefent Parlent, que toutz lez petitions baillez par lez ditz Communes, a dit tres haut & tres puiffant Prince le Duc de Gloucefter, Gardeyn d'Engleterre, en ceft prefent Parlement, foient refponduz & terminez dedeins ceft Roialme d'Engleterre, durant mefme cell' Parlement. Et fi afcuns petitions remaignount nient ref-

responduz & determinez, duraunt mesme cell Parlement, q'ils soient tenuz pur voides & de null effect; & que cest ordenaunce soit de force & tiegne lieux en chescun Parlement à tenir en cest Roialme d'Engleterre en temps a venir.—

Responsio. Soit advisée par le Roi.

Rotul. Parl. 4 Hen. VII. n. 25.

ITEM, die Veneris, Quarto die Decembris, anno supradicto, predictus Archiepiscopus declaravit, qualit' Ambassiatores Francie, intelligentes Dominum Regem & tres Status hujus Regni, cum ipsorum Ambassiatorum a rege nostro desideratis minime fore contentos, pecierunt a Rege licenciam animadvertendi Dominum suum Francor' Regem per unum ipsorum, sperantes, in bri' sufficienciorem & largiorem auctoritatem a dicto Francorum Rege habitur', qua possent ad nostri Regis complacentiam & utriusque Regnorum Anglie & Francorum commodum firmius concordare. Et quia appropinquante Festo Natalis Domini, ante quod festum, dictum negotium & alia quam plura bonum publicum hujus regni concernentia, in Parliamento predicto mota & desiderata, finiri & concludi minime poterant; idem Dominus Rex Anglie, presens Parliamentum suum usque vicesimum quintum diem Januarii tunc prox' futur' duxit prorogand', & illud realiter prorogavit: premuniens omnibus quorum interfuit in hac parte

e'endi

APPENDIX.

e'endi ap'id Weſtm', ad diem prediɛtum, locis conſuetis, quavis poſtpoſita excuſacionem, ad convocand' ſuper negociis ante diɛtis, & aliis quæ ex eor' co'ini aſſenſu pro bono publico, Domino concedente, contigerint ordinari.

Rot. Parl. 29 Hen. VI. Pars 2.

Soit as baille as Seigneurs.

To the Kyng our Soverain Lord.

PRAYEN the Commons, that where in your Parlement laſt holden at Weſtminſter, the Communaùlte of this your Roialme in the ſame Parlement aſſembled, accuſed and empeched, William De la Pole, thenne Duke of Suffolk, as well of divers grete, heynous, and deteſtable treaſons, as of many other fauxtees, deceites, and other untrue meſpriſions, by him doon and commyted: unto which accuſements and empechements, he being put to anſwere therto, gaue not anſwere ſufficient after the lawes of this your lande, as in the aɛtes and proceſſe hadde upon the ſaid accuſement and empechement, the tenour whereof herto is annexed more pleynly it appeareth; by cauſe whereof, jugement of atteyndre of the ſeid treaſons ought to have been given agenſt him, and he conviɛt of the ſeid meſpriſions after the cours of youre ſeid lawes; and foraſmuche as ſuch jugement agenſt him than was nought hadde, as juſtice after his merites

ites required.—Pleafe hit your Highneffe to graunte, ordeyne and eftablifh, by the avyfe and affent of the Lordes Spirituelx and Temporelx, in this prefent Parlement affembled, that by authorite of this *fame Parlement,* the faid William De la Pole be adjuged, demed, declared, publifhed, and reputed as a traytor to your, &c.

Dorfo. Le Roi s'advifera.

Addenda to Page xviii. of this Appendix.

After the confideration of which precedents, and others mentioned in the debate, and reading the orders made nineteenth of March, $167\frac{8}{3}$, and two and twentieth of May, one thoufand fix hundred eighty-five, concerning impeachments; and after long debate thereupon, and feveral things moved:

This queftion was propofed,

' Whether James Earl of Sarum and Henry Earl
' of Peterborough fhall be now difcharged from their
' bail?'

Then this previous queftion was put, ' Whether
' this queftion fhall be now put?'

It was refolved in the affirmative.

Then the main queftion was put, ' Whether
' James Earl of Salifbury and Henry Earl of
' Peterborough fhall be now difcharged from
' their bail?'

It was refolved in the affirmative.

' Leave having been given to any Lords, to enter
' their diflents, if the queftion was carried in
' the affirmative;

' And thefe Lords following do enter their
' diflents, in thefe reafons:

' 1. Be-

' 1. Becaufe we conceive it is a queftion not at all relating to the real debate before us; but urged upon us, not for the fake only of the two Lords mentioned.

' 2. Becaufe we ought to have examined precedents of pardons, to fee how far an impeachment was concerned, before we had adjudged the Lords difcharged; or whether an impeachment could be pardoned without particular mention in an act of grace; and what difference there is between an act of grace and an act of indemnity.

' 3. Becaufe we did not hear the Houfe of Commons, who are parties, and who in common juftice ought to have been heard before we had paffed this vote.'

' BOLTON.
' NORTH & GREY.
' STAMFORD.
' J. BRIDGWATER.
' BATHE.
' MACLESFELD.
' GRANVILLE. HERBERT.'

THE END.

www.ingramcontent.com/pod-product-compliance
Lightning Source LLC
Chambersburg PA
CBHW032139160426
43197CB00008B/707